LIVING AS A CHRISTIAN

A.W. TOZER

Compiled and Edited by James L. Snyder

LIVING

◦◦ AS A ◦◦

CHRISTIAN

TEACHINGS FROM FIRST PETER

Regal

From Gospel Light
Ventura, California, U.S.A.

Published by Regal
From Gospel Light
Ventura, California, U.S.A.
www.regalbooks.com
Printed in the U.S.A.

All Scripture quotations, unless otherwise indicated, are taken from the
King James Version. Other version used is *Phillips—The New Testament in Modern English*
Revised Edition, J. B. Phillips, Translator. © J. B. Phillips 1958, 1960, 1972.
Used by permission of Macmillan Publishing Co., Inc., 866 Third Avenue,
New York, NY 10022.

ISBN 978-1-61664-096-5

Rights for publishing this book outside the U.S.A. or in non-English languages are
administered by Gospel Light Worldwide, an international not-for-profit ministry.
For additional information, please visit www.glww.org, email info@glww.org, or write
to Gospel Light Worldwide, 1957 Eastman Avenue, Ventura, CA 93003, U.S.A.

CONTENTS

THE AMAZING CHRISTIAN

What is a Christian? The contemporary scene is flooded with all kinds of erroneous ideas of what it means to be a Christian, most taken from the culture around us. For some, the Christian is simply a cleaned-up person trying to do the best he can. Some have crafted a template into which they try to squeeze the Christian. But the Christian does not fit, and the result is a caricature, without any power or authority.

In this book, Dr. Tozer is writing to the Christian whose love and affection for Christ is the all-consuming passion of his life . . . every day. He is not writing about the carnal Christian who has not surrendered himself to Christ's rule in his life. Throughout this book, he makes one assumption: that he is talking to someone who has experienced a genuine conversion experience. He insists that we must have the utmost confidence in our conversion experience and trust the Holy Spirit to guide us day by day in the way that brings the most glory to the Christ who died for us. Tozer begins where most writers end. To him, conversion is not the end but rather the beginning of a wonderful walk of faith and trust and, yes, of works.

It was interesting to me to see Dr. Tozer's comment about Hebrews 11. Most of us look at that as the "faith chapter" of the Bible, but Tozer, in his inimitable way, calls it the "works chapter." Faith without works is dead, and there has to be a balance between what we believe and what we live. Nobody can walk far on only one foot—we need the balance of both feet, and Dr. Tozer gives us quite a spiritual balance as he describes from God's Word what the Christian walk is all about.

Certainly, we need to celebrate what we have been saved from. That should bring to us a great deal of praise and thanksgiving that God has saved us from a life of wretchedness. But, more important, we need to celebrate what we have been saved unto. The Christian walk is the forward walk. It is the "looking unto Jesus" that is most important. Every redeemed person has a specific destiny to fulfill. Discovering that destiny and fulfilling it in the power of the indwelling Holy Spirit is the joy of the Christian's daily walk.

We must start with Christ, continue with Christ and, finally, end with Christ. It is always Jesus Christ, our all in all; anything outside of Christ is not part of the Christian's life and walk.

Throughout the book, Dr. Tozer spends time developing the theme of salvation as God's master plan for man. The preciousness of God's plan of salvation reveals the value He places on man. Salvation is not a casual thing to God, and should not be thought of carelessly by us. To use a favorite Tozer illustration, it is not put a nickel in the slot, pull the lever, take a box of salvation and then go your separate way. Rather, what salvation does to the person who embraces Jesus Christ is nothing short of revolutionary, and his walk from that moment on is nothing short of miraculous.

This amazing Christian is the reflection of salvation's glory in the world around him. Not only is salvation a precious and wonderful thing, but also so is the Christian. Salvation is not an end in itself, but rather a plan for man to get back into the center of God's love and favor. Everything about the Christian reflects the glory of his salvation. All heaven looks with pride upon this curious creature called a Christian.

This Christian can withstand anything that comes against him, including heresy of all kinds that have infested the Church from the beginning. Tozer describes these heresies and how the Christian rises above them, including the blatant attack of Christianity's archenemy, the devil. It also includes the Christian's attitude toward persecution and suffering for the cause of Christ. This remarkable Christian is in the world, but he is not of it. Therefore, how he lives in front of the unsaved is crucial.

Because of the Christian's position in Christ, seated in the heavenlies, no matter what befalls, he is above all harm and can rest in the security of Jesus Christ, the victor. Dr. Tozer says, "No one, no thing, no circumstance can harm a good man." This "good man" is immortal, and when his destiny on earth has been completed, his destiny continues in what he has inherited through salvation.

James Snyder

TEACHINGS FROM FIRST PETER

THE CHRISTIAN
BELIEVES IN THINGS
HE CANNOT SEE

Whom having not seen, ye love; in whom, though now ye see him not,
yet believing, ye rejoice with joy unspeakable and full of glory.

1 PETER 1:8

Of all the apostles, Simon Peter, in my opinion, looms ahead of them all. His life and ministry are quite interesting to pursue. One of the most colorful of the disciples, he was the most vocally devoted to his Lord and ready to die for Him. I could raise some concern about some of his attitudes and actions revealed to us in Scripture, but down deep inside, Peter was radically committed to the Lord Jesus Christ, which is why I hold him in such admiration. He did not often know how to show his love, but after that mighty day of Pentecost (see Acts 2), Peter, along with the rest of the disciples, was never the same again. He became a mighty force for God.

His writings are not eloquent like those of the apostle Paul's, for he takes a rather down-to-earth approach to Christianity. His words do not rise up in moments of ecstasy and oratory as Paul's often did, but they have a way of presenting truth that the average Christian can grasp. By reading his epistles, I can almost hear him preaching simple and practical Bible sermons. In the language of the common man, Peter tells in his epistles about this amazing, indestructible Christian, of which he is a part, who believes even when he cannot see that in which he believes.

In 1 Peter 1:8, Peter begins his description of this amazing Christian. He uses two expressions very much alike except in tense: "whom having not seen" and "now ye see him not." "Having not seen" has to do with any possibility of seeing Him in the past, and "now ye see him not" has to do with any possibility of seeing Him now.

Christians, who are God's by sanctification of the Spirit and having been sprinkled with the blood of Christ, are believers in that which they cannot see and that which they have not seen. An old proverb says, "Seeing is believing." Of course, there is a kind of believing that must depend upon seeing. However, it is merely a conclusion drawn from the testimony of the senses. This is not New Testament believing at all. New Testament believing believes a report about things unseen, which is the difference between New Testament faith and every other kind of so-called believing.

These Christians believed in the invisible, another way of stating it, and this brings it close to Hebrews 11:27: "By faith he forsook Egypt, not fearing the wrath of the king: for he endured, as seeing him who is invisible." Abraham was able to endure because he was looking at the things that were invisible.

Being what we are, we pretty much trust what we can physically see; but if we could see all around us, if we could see the wonders, the invisible things of the creation, we would never be lonely for a moment and we would never doubt what is unseen. The invisible things are there, but they are simply not seen without faith. Abraham had faith and was able to carry on because he could see that which was not seen and could not be seen. And in so doing, these Christians mentioned in 1 Peter experienced the invisible so vividly and so satisfyingly that they were able to rejoice with joy unspeakable and full of glory.

Today we sing songs that are so dishonest that I sometimes hesitate to sing them. Yet when we sing the average hymn, if God Almighty compelled us to be entirely 100 percent honest, we simply could not sing them because their words would not be true of us.

Let me offer the words of a few hymns as examples. Here are the words of one song we sing often in our churches: "My faith looks up to Thee, Thou Lamb of Calvary, Savior divine!" It is a beautiful song written by Ray Palmer (1808–1887). When he wrote the last line—"O bear me safe above, a ransomed soul!" Palmer said, "I was so moved by what I was writing and what I was thinking about, that the last verse was written in a flood of tears." That man meant it, but I wonder how many of us mean it when we sing that hymn today? It is only by a charitable adaptation of the truth that we are able to sing most of the hymns we sing.

"Love Divine, All Loves Excelling," written by Charles Wesley (1707-1788), is another hymn we sing with very little meaning.

Love divine, all loves excelling,
Joy of heaven to earth come down;
Fix in us thy humble dwelling;
All thy faithful mercies crown!
Jesus, Thou art all compassion,
Pure unbounded love Thou art;
Visit us with Thy salvation;
Enter every trembling heart.

I remember an old camp meeting song popular years ago, "Like a Mighty Sea," written by A. I. Zelley:

Like a mighty sea, like a mighty sea,
Comes the love of Jesus sweeping over me;
The waves of glory roll, the shouts I can't control;
Comes the love of Jesus sweeping o'er my soul.

I can easily believe that the brother who wrote those words was so lost in the grace of God that when he said, "The waves of glory roll, the shouts I can't control," he was literally telling the truth. Yet, many who sing "the shouts I can't control" *can* control their shouts easier than they can control their lust and their temper.

If the average Christian were to sing, "The waves of glory roll, my tongue I can't control," he would be telling the truth. But to say, "The shouts I can't control" is to lie in the face of God Almighty. Yet we do an awful lot of lying. I suggest if you cannot feel it, do not sing it. Let us compromise and put it like this: let us sing it saying in our hearts, "Oh, God, it isn't true, but I want it to be true. It isn't so, Lord, but please make it so." I think God would understand and honor our desire.

If he or she is honest, the average Christian will sing, "See how I grovel here below, fond of these earthly toys," rather than sing, "The waves of glory roll, my shouts I can't control." How can we become the ones who sing in honesty "My shouts I can't control"?

The Christians Peter writes about saw the invisible, believed in it and rejoiced with "joy unspeakable and full of glory." I do not know how to tell you how to get it; I only know how they got it. They got it by believing in what they could not see, and that is the only way that you and I will ever have joy unspeakable and a shout that we cannot control.

Belief in Things Not Seen

The characteristic of a Christian that Peter is trying to establish here is that he believes in things he cannot see. This Christian believes in the invisible. He believes that the real world coexists with the physical world, touching this world and accessible to this world. There is never any contradiction between spirit and reality. The contradiction is between spirit and matter, never between the spiritual and the real. So the believer accepts and believes in a real world of which God is the King, an eternal kingdom, an eternal world, a spiritual and invisible world co-existing with and touching and accessible to this world. Heaven is not so far away that we must take a jet and continue through light years of travel to get to heaven. The average Christian thinks of heaven as being so far away, and only by accommodation do we sing about heaven being near and "glory coming down our souls to greet."

The eternal world of which God is the King is inhabited by immortal spirits and has taken our dead Christian loved ones for a little time out of our sight. That world is as real, more real, in fact, than the physical world with which we are so very familiar. There is a wonderful sense of coexisting in our world. This is not like the great vacuum gap between the stars in the heavens. You see a star in the heavens, and between that star and the next star are a few million light years of space. The visible world that is all around us is not separated from those invisible things.

It is a commonly known fact that two things of equal density cannot occupy the same place at the same time. But here is something we must remember on the other side: Two things that are not of equal density may coexist in the same place at the same time.

For instance, if you are sitting in front of your fireplace with the fire blazing, there would be two things coexisting—light and heat. They are not equal density; they are not mutually exclusive; they are mutually compatible and are the two things coming out of that fireplace.

Consider also the sun in the heaven above. Two things come from the sun at the same time, coexisting with each other: heat and light. We are warmed by the sun and we are lighted by the sun. Light and heat do not exclude each other; they are compatible and entwined with each other and live together. Therefore, the world below that God has made, which we call nature, and the world above that God has made, which He calls heaven, are coexistent.

Not only are they coexistent with each other, but they also touch each other and are accessible to each other so that God could put a ladder upon the earth and have its top reach the sky with angels ascending and descending. The one world is accessible to the other world either way; the gates swing both directions so that God could send His only begotten Son down and He could carry Stephen up. We can send our prayers up, and the answers can come down. The two worlds touch and are co-existent and accessible one to the other.

This Christian that Peter writes about believes in the invisible world. And this distinguishes him from every kind of materialism. During holiday seasons, our media boasts of the spiritual. However, after the season is over, they go back to materialism. Even while they are celebrating the spiritual, they do it in a materialistic way. The Christian, however, sharply distinguishes from all kinds of materialism. He does not put a lot of value in what he sees. He does not limit his belief to only what he is able to touch with his hands. He endures, seeing the invisible. The immaterialist is not ghostly and phantom, but spiritual. That which is spiritual has real existence but is spirit instead of matter. The Christian believes that and lives in the light of it, which distinguishes him forever from all brands of materialism.

It also distinguishes him from all kinds of superstition and idolatry. The idolater also believes in the invisible, but the difference is that a Christian is one whose faith in the invisible has been corrected and chastened and purified by divine revelation.

A heathen can kneel down before a stone and if he is an intelligent heathen, you might ask him, "Why do you worship that stone?" He could answer, "I don't; I worship the deity resident in the stone."

The Greeks used to kneel in front of Mount Olympus, and if you said to them, "Why are you worshiping Mount Olympus?" they would say, "We do not worship the mountain; we worship the gods in the mountain." Even today, there are those who will kneel before statues in churches, and if you ask them, "Why do you worship that image?" they say, "We don't worship that image, we worship God of whom that image reminds us."

The Christian's View of the Invisible

It is entirely possible to be a believer in the invisible and not be a Christian. Many people fall into this category. But it is not possible to be a Christian and not believe in the invisible. It is possible to believe that there is some kind of spooky world somewhere that must be placated with rabbit's feet, strange sayings, chains around our neck and medallions and all sorts of things. That is a belief in the invisible, but it is a pagan, erroneous belief.

When Jesus Christ came and brought life and immortality to light through the Gospels, He stood up, opened His mouth and talked to us, correcting that false and sinful belief in superstitious things by telling us what the real world is. He was the only one who had ever been there to come back and tell us. Abraham died, and his body sleeps in the cave of the field of Machpelah, while his spirit is with God; but he has never been back to tell us what it is like. Jesus, however, has been there from eternity, and when He came to earth, He told us of things of heaven and chided us because we did not accept what He said.

So the Christian is not a materialist that only believes in the validity of all material things. He is not an idolater, believing only vaguely in the existence of another world. He believes in what he has been taught by the One who had been there and came across the threshold into our world, smelling of myrrh and aloes out of the ivory palaces (see Ps. 45:8), fragrant from the presence of the eternal King.

The Christian's Trust in the Invisible

Not only does a Christian believe in the invisible world but he also counts on it. He acts, plans and lives as one who counts on the reality of the invisible. On the opposite side, the man of the earth does not believe in another world, or if he believes in it, he nods dutifully toward the belief in another world, but he does not let it change his plans any. He acts just the same as if there were no other world. He lays his plans precisely the same as if there were no invisible world, and he continues to live as if heaven is a myth and does not exist.

But the Christian counts on the other world, so that the invisible presence of God in His eternal kingdom, and the spirits made perfect in the holy church of the first-born, and the Holy Ghost and the invisible world actually influence his life. The invisible actually shapes his plans, determines his habits, comforts, consoles and supports him.

It is a comforting thought that God is near us. It is a comforting thought that there are invisible worlds near us. It consoles us to know that when Jesus prayed in the garden of Gethsemane, angels came to comfort Him, and He could have had legions of angels by His side. Nothing has changed. As the poem "The Kingdom of God" by Francis Thompson (1859-1907) proclaims:

The angels keep their ancient places—
Turn but a stone and start a wing!
'Tis ye, 'tis your estranged faces,
That miss the many-splendored thing.

Our unbelieving hearts have missed "the many-splendored thing." Angels are still here. Our friends on the other side of the ecclesiastical stone hedge are great for angels and celebrate the angelic host almost any time, day or night. But I have a sneaking suspicion there is a closer relation between their concept of angels and the pagan concept of Mount Olympus than there is of the New Testament concept. Because they go in big for Saint Angels, we do not need to turn our backs on angels and say they are not here. They are here, and Jesus said about the little child, "Take heed that ye despise not one of these little ones; for I say unto you, that in heaven their angels do always behold the face of my Father which is in heaven" (Matt. 18:10).

Because pagan religion has mixed with Christianity and has created a perverted and false view of the angelic ministry is no reason for turning our backs on the whole thing. Because the Muslims pray falsely and dutifully five times a day is no reason for me not to pray. Because the Mormons have their Book of Mormon is no reason I am going to kick the Bible out into the alley. Because the Christian Scientists meet in a church building is no reason why I am going tear some church building down. The fact of counterfeit should never force us to throw out the real thing.

Look at a real quarter and you read the words "Liberty, In God We Trust." On the other side is "United States of America,

E Pluribus Unum, Quarter Dollar." I have never to my knowledge handled a counterfeit quarter, but if I had a counterfeit quarter and somebody pitched it back to me and said it was counterfeit, I would not take out all my quarters and throw them out in the back yard. Just because there is counterfeit abroad is no reason why I should reject the truth. If some people make too much of angels, that is no reason why I should get even with them and speak too little of them.

Quaker educator Thomas Kelly pointed out that we live on two planes: the plane of the natural and the plane of the spiritual. That is why a Christian is such a wonderful, weird, strange and puzzling creature. He is both animal and spirit, insisting upon living for the spiritual while down here in his mortal body, making a Christian a funny fellow.

Take for example, two men living on the same street together at number 1631 and number 1633, side by side. They are as different as night and day. One is a good-natured, easygoing, relaxed, downright old sinner on his way to hell but does not believe it. He is easy to get along with, bothers nobody, is friendly and waves when he goes down the street. He is a sinner, an Esau, a good-natured rebel on his way to hell.

Living alongside of him is a Christian, one that has been born again and has been given the blessed Holy Ghost as the wedding ring, but he has his troubles. He weeps when there is nothing to weep about and is moody when there is no reason. He is preoccupied when somebody is standing next to him wanting to talk. When the man next door cannot keep his radio off he's worried about whether there has been bombing overseas. He may put his Bible under his arm and start off somewhere to a street meeting or to a prayer meeting. He is not as comfortable a fellow as the sinner is, and he does not act quite the same.

Why? Because the sinner lives on only one plane—the physical—and the Christian lives on two planes—the physical and the spiritual. In his body, he is down here in the flesh; but in his spirit, he is up yonder with God. And the result is that he is not as comfortable to be around as he might be. I have always said prophets are never comfortable people to have around, but they are indispensable if we are not going to rot.

The Christian's Preoccupation with the Invisible

It is characteristic of the Christian to be preoccupied with the invisible. Let me use the Lord's Supper as an illustration. What is a sacrament? A sacrament is where the invisible meets and touches the visible. Eternal meets and touches the temporal. The Lord's Supper is a sacrament wherein we use the material as a thin garment to disguise the spiritual, and we use the temporal as a plate upon which we serve the eternal. That has always been the belief of the Christian.

There are two schools of thought that center on the sacrament of the Lord's Supper. The first is that the elements actually become visible—the invisible becomes visible—and that when you take the bread from the tray, you are touching consciously and lifting the very body that Mary gave to Jesus. That seems unworthy of a serious answer.

The second school of thought believes the invisible is present in, underneath and behind the visible, and I believe in that.

Wherever faith has eyes to see, there is a smiling presence of the Son of God. I believe that in the Lord's Supper, in the bread and the wine, we can trace it, we can know where it came from; we bought it. There is nothing magical about it. It could be fed to the birds; any sinner could drink the cup; there is nothing magical about it, but it is an object lesson. It sets forth in material terms the spiritual. It sets forth in temporal terms the eternal. And wherever faith is present, we touch and handle things unseen.

An illustration of this would be in the celebration of the Lord's Table. Even in the Early Church, some Christians became so engrossed with material things that they failed to recognize the spiritual. They drank the wine and enjoyed it and ate the bread and were full, but in so doing they did not have faith in the invisible. They were not discerning the Lord's body (see 1 Cor. 11:29-30).

Throughout the Scripture, especially in the writings of the apostle Paul, the believers were warned about eating and drinking the Lord's Supper as a mere carnal thing. For many it became just a meal set before them to enjoy. This materialistic thinking grieved God. The Lord's Supper is more than just material elements; rather, for the man or woman of faith it is through this material gateway that we reach the spiritual.

The spiritual and the invisible and the eternal are right here. Faith recognizes that. This amazing Christian that Peter writes about puts his faith in the invisible, in that which he has not seen, so that the invisible has become visible.

2

THE CHRISTIAN UNDERSTANDS THE TRUTH ABOUT SALVATION

Of which salvation the prophets have inquired and searched diligently, who prophesied of the grace that should come unto you: Searching what, or what manner of time the Spirit of Christ which was in them did signify, when it testified beforehand the sufferings of Christ, and the glory that should follow. Unto whom it was revealed, that not unto themselves, but unto us they did minister the things, which are now reported unto you by them that have preached the gospel unto you with the Holy Ghost sent down from heaven; which things the angels desire to look into.

1 PETER 1:10-12

Throughout the Bible three major truths divide up nicely into singular truth, rare truth and reassuring truth. An understanding of this trinity of truth is essential in comprehending the dynamics of salvation.

Truth is singular because it is not much mentioned in the Bible. Salvation is such a heavenly and mysterious thing that the very prophets who foretold it did not understand and actually searched and inquired diligently concerning the salvation they were writing about with passion. They knew only that they wrote of some favored people who were to come, who were to receive remarkable, fabulous wealth at the hand of a kind and gracious God, but they did not understand it fully.

Then there is the rare truth that the Old Testament prophets had the Spirit of Christ. Our salvation is known and talked about in heaven and is admired by the unfallen angels. It is not a recent thing, not even relatively recent, but very old. It is the theme of all the inspired prophets since the world began. This all leads us to reassuring truth.

A Singular Truth

We must begin with singular truth, which greatly influenced the Old Testament prophets. We read:

> Of which salvation the prophets have inquired and searched diligently, who prophesied of the grace that should come unto you: Searching what, or what manner of time the Spirit of Christ which was in them did signify, when it testified beforehand the sufferings of Christ, and the glory that should follow. Unto whom it was revealed, that not unto themselves, but unto us they did minister the things, which are now reported unto you by them that have preached the gospel unto you with the Holy Ghost sent down from heaven; which things the angels desire to look into (1 Pet. 1:10-12).

I think we can learn a lot about biblical inspiration here, of which there are many theories. I do not believe that evangelical truth necessarily must accept any one theory of inspiration as long as we believe that the holy men of God spoke as they were moved by the Holy Ghost. "For verily I say unto you, till heaven and earth pass, one jot or one tittle shall in no wise pass from the law, till all be fulfilled" (Matt. 5:18). This, I believe, fulfills the requirements for belief concerning inspiration of Scripture.

Some believe that the inspired writers wrote only of what they knew. They were simply religious reporters reporting intelligently and spiritually on what they knew and then exhorted and consoled and rebuked, giving application to what they knew to the hearts of the people. That does not go far enough. The fact is that sometimes the prophets were moved to speak of things they did not understand. They heard the Spirit's voice witnessing within them about wondrous things and they spoke what they heard, but they did not know of what they spoke. It was a relatively easy matter for a prophet to understand when God revealed that Babylon should fall, that Israel should be taken captive or that Ahab should die and the dogs should lick his blood, or any of the scores of other prophecies concerning historic events. That was a relatively easy thing, and every prophet understood it.

Suppose I had a prophetic foresight that all of the United States faced destruction by a nuclear bomb and I was to write it down. I could understand my own writing. It would be a question of visualizing the destruction of that vast city. Many of the Old Testament prophecies were on the rational level and could be understood easily by the prophets who prophesied. But when they entered the wondrous golden world of grace, mercy, salvation, incarnation, resurrection, atonement, ascension and the sending of the Holy Ghost, and the new birth and the bringing to being of a people made again in the image of God, the prophets staggered. They could not get it. It was simply a question of historic fact; it was a question of marvelous spiritual understanding, and they did not have it. So they prophesied about others, and they were included, of course, but that was not what was in their mind at the moment. They were prophesying for the future, and they died not having received the promise; but the prophecies were perpetuated by divine inspiration and by translation as we have them today in our Bible.

They heard the Spirit's voice speaking within them, and they uttered forth what they heard. As prophets, they were able to prophesy; but as individual men, they had to examine and search. I wonder: What did they search? Did they search some other prophet's writing? Did they search their own heart? Or did they seek in the sense that the Scripture says, "Seek and ye shall find"? Peter does not say specifically what to seek, and I'm sure every preacher and teacher has his own interpretation on this subject.

It is usually the case in the Word of God that there are a multitude of applications, so that if one man says it means this, and another man says it means that, and three others say it means some other thing, they are not contradicting each other; they may easily be complementing each other's interpretation. I have no objection to various interpretations provided they do not say, "Accept my interpretation or I rule you out." That mindset is too narrow and legalistic.

The prophets prophesied of things to come. It is a wonderful truth and a curious one that the prophets reported on things they themselves did not understand.

A Rare Truth

Rare truth is that of which there is not much directly stated in either Old or New Testament, but it is here in 1 Peter 1:10-12 bluntly stated in unmistakable language. The Old Testament prophets had the Spirit of Christ, but the word "had" is not good enough, for it says, "the Spirit of Christ, which was in them." Note that the preposition is "in."

This destroys what some people call the geographical interpretation of the Holy Ghost. I would call it the prepositional interpretation of the Holy Ghost. There are those who bear down very heavily on the words "on" and "with" and "in." They say about the Holy Spirit that He was "on" the Old Testament saints but not "in" them. That He was "with" the apostles before Pentecost but not "in" or "on" them; after Pentecost, He got "in" the people. That makes preaching easy, because all you have to do is look for the prepositions in the Word of God and hook your little comment on them.

I have never been able to believe that God played in the marketplace and that He built His truth out of curious little blocks. No, the Bible does not tell us that, but only that the Holy Ghost was "on" men. But it says here that He was "in" them. That little preposition "in" may ruin some people's theology because they believe the Old Testament prophets and saints never had the Holy Ghost; that He was only "on" them. They believe He came and rested upon them; the Dove lighted on the roof but never came inside the dwelling place. They say you have to believe that, or else they will not admit you into their little narrow field of thought. But in the New Testament it says He came "with them," and they quote Jesus as saying, "he is now with you but shall be in you" meaning Himself as the "with," and then when the Spirit came at Pentecost He filled them, and so the Spirit was "in them."

I believe the Holy Ghost was both "on" and "in" the Old Testament prophets, and I believe the Holy Ghost comes on and in New Testament Christians. I believe that the Holy Ghost was in the Old Testament prophets, for Peter says so, and I must take Peter's word for it in spite of the commentators.

There is honest confusion here, and I do not want to get ironical about this, though I fear an ironical quality has crept in. But there seems to be honest confusion on this subject for a number of reasons.

Looking Past the Simple and the Practical

First, it results from letting the element of curiosity crowd out the element of practicality. If Bible teachers could only remember that the "holy men spake as they were moved by the Holy Ghost" and gave us divinely inspired truth, and never for one remote moment meant to give us anything to satisfy our intellectual curiosity, they would realize that the prophets meant to give us truth to transform spirit and soul and bring us into holy living and holy believing. They never intended that we should have theological baby rattles to entertain ourselves.

I have been to Bible conferences and heard teachers of many schools of religious Christian interpretation give the impression that they were proud of their ability to bring things out, both old and new, and particularly, new. And after they had settled the hash of the ordinary, simple interpretation of the thing, they gave you some curious interpretation. They had enjoyed the theology from a curious standpoint.

I believe that this type of thing will lead us astray. As soon as we accept the doctrine or the idea that the Bible is a book of theological toys to be played with by tender saintlings, we have missed the purpose of the Scripture and face the danger of slipping into false doctrine before very long. For the Bible was given to us not to satisfy our curiosity but to sanctify our personality.

Forcing the Interpretation

The second reason that has resulted in this confusion about the Holy Spirit being "on" and "in" and "with," and so on, is the carnal urge to rightly divide. Rightly dividing the Word of Truth turns out to be anemic and usually bleeds to death in the hands of the man who holds it. Then he carries a dead text around with him and rams it down everybody's throat. The carnal urge to "rightly divide" arises from intellectual pride. And that is what we call trying too hard.

In trying to understand the Scripture, we are in grave danger of trying too hard. It is rare that we can pull our belt tight to the last notch, grit our teeth and say, "I am going to get this." God never has very much place for old Adam. He bid old Adam good-bye and said that the end of all flesh had come before him. God has never put any confidence in the flesh from that hour down to this.

33

When the Old Testament priests went into the inner sanctum to offer sacrifices, they did not wear wool clothing, because wool made them perspire. I imagine God was saying to the Jewish priesthood, "Now, do not mistake perspiration for inspiration. Your human perspiration will not glorify me; therefore, wear linen clothing so you can keep cool and serve Me scripturally and spiritually but calmly and coolly, and don't imagine that by trying hard you'll get anywhere." There is a lot of paganism in climbing Jacob's ladder with white knuckles and tired muscles. The Lord wants to kill all that and let the Holy Ghost take over.

When Jesus sweated blood in the garden of Gethsemane, it was quite another matter. That was not old Adam trying too hard. That was the Holy Ghost coming upon a man until He nearly burnt Him up. That was the prayer spirit laboring on the man until it nearly killed the man. I believe in that, but I also believe that theologians who push too hard usually fail to see the point, because they are not relaxed.

The world of sports often gives us good illustrations of this. A young batter with an average of .300 to .325 suddenly goes into a slump and could not hit a pumpkin if it came across the plate. His slump is because of his inexperience. When he gets up to bat he tenses up and tries too hard. Finally, he says, "What's the use . . . I couldn't hit a basketball." Suddenly, he starts to hit again because he is not tense and he is not trying too hard. I have met many saints who are just trying too hard.

At a New Year's Watch Night service many years ago, one very godly man jumped to his feet, gripped his hands together and in a spasm of dynamic determination told us his plans for the New Year and how he was going to serve God. My quiet, saintly friend beside me touched my arm and whispered, "Brother Everett is screwing his violin strings too tight. He won't be able to keep it up for the year." The prophecy proved true.

You can throw your flesh into the effort, and with strong religious determination break your teeth and batter your own head black and blue but never get anywhere. You can do that in theology too. The simplest explanation of any text is just what it says. Just read it, get on your knees and take it at its plainest meaning. As Mark Twain quipped: "Most people are bothered by those passages of Scripture they don't understand, but for me I have always noticed that the passages that bother me are those I do understand." You will have time enough following the text that you understand without seeking piously underneath the surface to bring up some esoteric meaning that God never put there.

Once, while preaching in Dr. A. B. Simpson's old church, The Gospel Tabernacle in New York City, down off Times Square, I said, merely as a matter of passing, "The angels are pure spirit and the animals are flesh; but man, this wondrous being, is both spirit and flesh." I then went on to something else. Afterward, a man with a face like a mask, cold eyes and expressionless face, said, "What did you say about the beast not having a spirit?"

I could tell he had taken that argument to all the preachers that visited New York since 1897, and he said, "Did God not make this covenant with all flesh?" Then I saw what I was into. At first, I treated him as a brother and tried to reason with him. Finally, I saw it was no use, and I said, "I perceive, sir, that you are a theological mechanic and more concerned with the letter than with the spirit. I worship the Most High God . . . goodbye," and I left him. He came back to all the meetings but he never bothered me anymore.

This man had taken from somewhere the idea that a dog has a spirit and that when God made a covenant with Adam, He included the dog. But it is all very silly, and if it is true, it does not mean anything. What do I care about horses, sheep, dogs and mountain lions? God never said to go into the world and preach the gospel to my horses. He died for people. He came to seek that which was lost, and we are the lost ones. When He came to earth and took on flesh, it was not the flesh of the beast but the flesh of the man; and it was a man that went up to Calvary, not a dog or bear. So if there is some hope for the beast, let there be hope.

The simple truth is that the Old Testament prophets had the Spirit of Jesus, and that is a very rare truth. The Spirit of Christ, which was in them, is here in the Bible, and they prepared the world for the Advent of the Savior because it was the Savior Himself in them. It was the Spirit of the Savior in them, prophesying, and they witnessed the Christ in type and symbol and historic situation and in the writings of the prophets. This explains why Christians love the Old Testament.

You may have wondered why you like the Old Testament so when the New Testament is your book. You can read the Old Testament, mark it and love it, and yet you know it belonged to an ancient dispensation and the New Testament is your book. The New Testament is not your book any more than the Old was. You cannot separate one from the other; they are an organic whole; the Spirit of Christ was in the Old Testament, and Christ is in the New Testament, and you have one and the same thing. There are passages in the Old Testament that do not refer to you and yet you feel an affinity for them. Read the book of Deuteronomy, which has to do almost wholly with Israel, and yet your heart warms and leaps and rejoices when you read it, and you mark passages and say, "I wonder why? Why do I love the Old Testament?" It is because the Spirit of Christ, which is in them, did testify; and you, who are born again, recognize the same Spirit that dwells in your breast in some measure, at least, and there is an affinity there. That is why the Old Testament should be read and preached today.

A Reassuring Truth

The third truth is a reassuring truth that redemption is famous in heaven and was famous in ancient times, and the plan of God to redeem the fallen race excited wonder and admiration among the very angels, which things angels desire to look into. I do not know how much they ever found out, but the angels were stirred with desire to know this wondrous redemption of mankind.

Why did the angels admire so greatly this truth? I believe it is for three reasons because of the being that is to be redeemed. If we could ever make people see three things about themselves, I think we could settle many of our problems. One is what wonderful creatures they are; second, what hopelessly sinful creatures they are; and third, what great hope there is in Christ. If we take the attitude that we are sinful and then begin to tramp ourselves down to the level of the gopher and the rat, or we take the idea that we are not sinful, and we deny that we have sinned, and we push ourselves up, both are true.

We are made in the image of God, and only a little lower than the angels and are to be higher than the angels. That is what we were and that is what we potentially are. But without the new birth and redemption and forgiveness and cleansing, we will find our place in that hell reserved for the devil and his fallen angels. Those two truths are not contradictory; they are two sides of the same truth. Mankind was made in God's image, and God, for that reason, sent His Son to die for us. Therefore, nobody ever ought to think low of himself but remember how humble and little and sinful and hopeless and broken he is before God.

We keep these two thoughts in suspension that though we were in the image of God, we stained our souls and ruined ourselves and brought judgment, hell and death upon us. Then God, for Christ's sake, saves us, redeems us for another's work and merit and restores us again to the image of God, and we shall one day stand a little higher than we anciently stood in the loins of our forefather Adam.

Those are wonderful truths, and they are reassuring truths. The angels are interested in this wonderful being called man.

The second reason is the astonishing mercy of God. If God gave us our just deserts, not one of us would be alive. A kind-faced woman that has spent her lifetime looking after children and then her grandchildren, and living the best she knew how, would be in hell too. And the honest businessman that never cheated in his life and is upright, good and honest and a worthy citizen would be in hell too. Everybody above the age of accountability belongs there, and whoever denies that he does, will go there.

Oh, the astonishing mercy of God that He should come to us because of what we were in Adam! Made in the image of God, we went down lower and further than we would have gone.

Oh, the grace and mercy of God that we should be saved! And that is why the angels stood with open eyes and said, "How can it be that such creatures as they should be treated as they are by the great God who loved them?"

The third reason, and this is the most important, is because of the one—Jesus Christ our Lord—who would rescue us. As we see these angels looking with reverent wonder and these prophets who prophesied since the world began wondering what it was all about and dreaming and hoping they might know, we can only say that our foundation stands sure. It is not a new religion; not Mrs. Eddy in a fit; not Father Divine with his old bald head and his angels and concubines; not Joseph A. Smith and his curious plates dug up under an apple tree. But before the world began, this was in the mind of God. Ancient as the sun and before the sun burned in the heavens, it was in the mind of God to redeem you and me. Angels desired to look into it.

An old saint of God whom I once knew lived a rather simple life and refused to say things that were not true. Unlike him, many Christians boast that they never have a doubt. The hypocrites. They do have doubts, but they will not admit it. This old man of God once testified, "I admit that I have doubts sometimes. I'll hear an argument or somebody will bounce an idea, and it'll stun me for a little. When I have such doubts I always dive down to the bottom and examine the foundation of my faith, and every time I've done it I've always come to the surface singing, 'How firm a foundation, ye saints of the Lord, is laid for your faith in his excellent Word.'"

How firm a foundation, ye saints of the Lord,
Is laid for your faith in His excellent Word!
What more can He say than to you He hath said,
You, who unto Jesus for refuge have fled?
—John Rippon (1751-1836)

The Christian knows that he is saved, even though many things about his salvation are beyond his comprehension, but not beyond his trust. The truth he hangs on to has withstood centuries of attack without wavering. Standing upon this foundation, the Christian never wavers about his salvation but bows his head in humble appreciation of the amazing grace of God.

3

THE CHRISTIAN
IS REDEEMED FROM
A FOOLISH WAY
OF LIFE

Forasmuch as ye know that ye were not redeemed with corruptible things, as silver and gold, from your vain conversation received by tradition from your fathers; but with the precious blood of Christ, as of a lamb without blemish and without spot.

1 PETER 1:18-19

Peter offers this beautiful symbolism of Jesus Christ as a lamb—a sacrificed lamb. He says, "Ye were redeemed." "Redeemed" means "loosed," not in the sense that you would loose a man bound to a post or loose a horse, but loosed in the legal sense of being freed from legal bondage. It is in the sense that a slave is loosed, is legally declared free. And Peter said, "You are loosed from the vain conversation."

Those who insist so religiously on the text, the letter and syllables, of the *King James Version* ought to listen sometimes to some preachers untangling the *King James* translation for modern listeners. For example, "vain conversation" does not mean what it means now. "Vain" means foolish and "conversation" means a manner of life. So what Peter said is, "For as much as ye know that ye were not redeemed with corruptible things as silver and gold from your foolish way of life . . ."

Foolish Living

This is a way of life that is morally foolish. It is the sinner's way of life, but God calls it a foolish way, an empty way. It is foolish for several reasons.

No Thought of God

The sinner's way is foolish because it neglects to give God His proper place. Any way of life, any attitude, any political philosophy, any moral philosophy or speculative philosophy, any kind of thinking in any sphere of human thought or life, any standard of morals adopted or followed by any people, however loosely, that does not give God His proper place is declared by the Lord God Himself to be foolish and empty.

People around us are foolish. Men who went out and got themselves pepped up during a holiday and then the next day suffered with an aching head were not so bad as they were just foolish. It is foolish to treat your body like that. They are doing a morally foolish thing because they do not consider God. No man who has God before his mind would ever swill poison liquor down his throat. Therefore, what people do is foolish.

In efforts of evangelism, some people try to make sinners out of everybody in the sense that they make them out to be vicious and low and wicked. That is not true. There are sinners who will certainly perish and spend their eternity in hell who are nevertheless courteous, kind, friendly gentlemen, and you would consider it a privilege to live next door to them. They are good neighbors, and thoughtful, but they are living without a thought of God in their minds. Their way is a foolish way of life because it is a godless way of life.

It is not always a morally low way of life, for there are levels of wickedness. But it is a way that does not consider God, and the Bible says it is foolish and ignores reason, for righteousness always has reason on its side. That was one of the teachings of Plato, that every man reasonably wanted to do the right thing, only that man made mistakes in deciding what the right things were. Ignoring reason was one of the basic tenets of the great Greek thinker. He was thinking, of course, of finer thinking people, but the great masses do not think too much. Reason is always on the side of righteousness.

When it comes to whether I should do something this way or that way, and the first way is wrong, but the second way is right, reason is always on the side of right. It is always illogical to do the wrong thing. Peter said that it is a foolish, illogical way to live, because it ignores God, ignores reason and disregards the moral lessons of history. Some people picture history as an old fellow with an old-fashioned quill pen writing lessons.

Even history is not always accurate. Voltaire (1694-1778) once said, "History is a pack of lies we play on the dead." That was a cynic's statement. The truth is, much can be learned from history. One thing we can learn is that it is always better to be righteous and it is always worse to be evil, to live without a thought of God before our minds. Ignoring moral reasoning is a fool's way of life.

No Thought of a Final Reckoning

And then the sinner's way of life is foolish because it assumes there is no final reckoning. It is like the man who plunges into some activity unaware or refusing to consider that someday he is going to have to pay up. Or like the man or woman who dances into the gray dawn and then fills up with stimulants, goes on dancing into the next dawn and beats himself up and abuses himself. They are having a type of fun but they are fools because they are not considering that there is a day of reckoning. There will be a time when angry Mother Nature will say, "Pay up."

The sinner's way is foolish because he does not believe there is a final reckoning, or if he believes it, he foolishly disregards it, assuming he is just going to be able to shuffle off this mortal coil without getting a reckoning and accounting. Well, he is not.

No Thought of the Invisible, Real World

The way of the sinner is foolish because it assumes that man is a one-world being. If there is anything I'm committed to it is that man lives on two planes, this world and the world above, the physical and the spiritual, the natural and the divine. Man is not made for one world only, but for two. He is made for this world now and the next world later. The sinner's way of life takes for granted this life and does not expect to face another world. This person jokes about this world being so terrible because you do not get out of it alive; that is very tragic when you consider that there is another world, but sinners act as if there is not.

The Christian is wise because he has considered the second world. He is wise because he takes into account that he must make a reckoning. He is wise because he has taken into account the moral lessons of history. He has not ignored reason but has given God His right place, allowing himself to be chastened with memories and knowledge of how others lived and what they paid for wrong living.

Vetted by Tradition

Peter says this way of life is received by tradition from our fathers, and the power of this way of life over us derives from two sources. One source is the approval of the ages. What our fathers did, we are inclined to think is right.

As a young preacher in West Virginia, I preached against tobacco. I still hate it as much as I did then, but I have sense enough to know that it is only a pimple on the body of morality. So I do not preach against tobacco, although I hate it. But in those days, I attacked anything that did not look good, and tobacco was one. I used to tell them they were dirty if they used it and could not be Christians. Do you know the response to that kind of preaching? White-faced anger. "Do you mean to tell me that my old father, who smoked and chewed until he died, and my grandmother, who smoked a clay pipe until she died, all perished?"

They were sanctifying the ways of their parents and they were on the cool end of a hot stick, which is smoking, because they liked the taste of it, but mainly because it was received as tradition from their fathers. It was sanctified by generation after generation of incense burners, and they did not want me to say a word about it. Not for their sakes, but because it seemed to be reflecting on the traditions of their fathers. I have learned better, and I preach Christ now.

People will justify anything if their fathers did it. Peter said you received this way of life by traditions of your father.

What Comes Naturally

Then the second source that this way of life stems from, or rather gets its power from, is what accords with the fallen tendencies of the human heart. Whatever accords with the fallen tendencies of the human heart you always do without much trouble.

If you do what comes naturally, you will be doing the way of the flesh; you will be doing that which is outside of the normal bodily functions. For there is a certain basic physical naturalness that even our Lord Jesus Christ had. It is perfectly natural to eat; it is perfectly natural to sleep, and so on. I am talking about an immoral kind of life that stems out of fallen nature, and that is easy to do.

For example, it is easy for a child to lie. I remember my first lie and how easy it was and how it got me out of a jam. It was Christmas, and my poor mother, God bless her memory, tried to get something for us children, if nothing but a popcorn ball. This time she found a Barlow knife. I got a Barlow knife, and I thought that was wonderful. When it was time to go back to school, they surrounded me and asked me what I got for Christmas. I felt chagrined to tell them I got a Barlow knife, and nothing else. Therefore, I used my imagination and fixed myself up with the nicest bunch of Christmas presents you ever heard of, and I got out of an embarrassing position by telling a lie.

That came naturally; I did not have to work at it. All I had to do was just open my mouth and nature took its course. Because we have these fallen tendencies, the foolish way of life is easy for us. It is always hard to teach a child to be good; let him alone and he will not be good.

You say, "But my little darling is good naturally." You are going to be surprised one of these days. Your disillusionment is coming; your little darling is one of Adam's wild beasts. And if you did not teach him to be good, he would never be good. If you did not teach him to wash, he would be so dirty you would have to fumigate him once a week. And if you did not teach him to tell the truth, he would lie to music. We are alike in things like that, and the reason your children are good is because you are good and you are teaching them to be good. Do not get it wrong, they did not inherit any goodness; you taught them; and that is to your credit, not theirs. And in turn, by the grace of God, we teach the next generation to be good.

People have to be taught to be good, for they will be bad without teaching, because we all receive it from our fathers by tradition, and it accords with the fallen tendencies of our heart. The honest businessman who conducts his affairs in an honest way is doing what he has learned to do. It would be the natural thing for him to reach out and rake in what he can get his hands on. But he has been trained and taught by religion and morals to be different.

Disentangled from the Sin Life

From this fallen way of life we are set free; we are redeemed. A Christian has been delivered from this way of life and from the moral magnetism of those entanglements.

A man once told about some sheep dying during a midwinter in Niagara River. Some of them had died upstream in Niagara, and they either would fall in or be thrown into Niagara River. It was very cold, but the tempestuous Niagara was not frozen, and it carried these dead sheep over the falls. Before the sheep went over the falls, the bald eagles would gather and dive down and ride these carcasses and tear out their flesh. One great eagle after another would fly upstream, land on one, tear with her talons, pull with her great sharp beak, get herself a mouth full of meat and gulp it. Then when they were about to go over the falls they would leap up gracefully on their broad wings and circle back and repeat the same thing over again.

As it was getting colder, one eagle made a mistake. She rode a little too long the last time, and her talons froze into the wool. When she, confident in her self-assurance, spread her great broad wings to take flight, her talons were frozen into the wool of the sheep and she plunged over to her death along with the carcass she had been feeding on. If somebody could have untangled her talons from the wool, it would have been a kind of redemption, a release.

God has provided a moral release from the tradition of our fathers, the foolish way of life that we see all around us. And it has been done by the act of God in redemption, involving the payment of a ransom for tomorrow. It is not a physical captivity, though it has physical implications for sinners, but it is legal in moral aspects. The ransom price had to be a moral ransom price. It had to be the blood of the Holy One, holy enough for God to accept. So that moral price was paid, and Peter says, "It was not silver or gold." If I were a slave in a market somewhere in Arabia or the Old South, and I was worth $200 or $5,000, depending upon my age and size and ability, someone might come with a pocket full of gold and buy me and then set me free. Bought free with money, with silver and gold. But when your bondage is not physical, but moral, you cannot buy off moral slaves with money.

So Peter said, "Ye were not redeemed with corruptible things, as silver and gold . . . but with the precious blood of Christ." This blood of the Lamb is precious because of what it means to God and because of what it means and what it meant to our Lord Jesus Christ, the deathless man who volunteered to die. God does not use words carelessly, and He called the blood of the Lamb precious. And it is precious for what it did for men.

Two men were traveling through the mountains and were overcome by what is called a Nor'wester, one of those sudden terrible storms. The temperature plunged to below zero and the blizzard began with high winds. A man, however well clothed, can simply die in that. He gets sleepy and wants to rest, never to wake up again.

So these two men were traveling together when the temperature suddenly plunged. It was becoming so cold that it was brutal and dangerous. They found themselves a little shelter by a little depression in the rock and they looked at each other and said, "A few hours of this and we're finished."

"Yes," one man said, "we're finished; we can't stand this; we'll be found dead here in the morning."

"Well," the other replied, "do you suppose we could start a fire?"

His companion said, "Let's try."

So they hurried around with numb fingers and gathered some sticks and leaves from out from under the overhanging rock, got themselves a few little shavings of wood, then they went for their matches, very few and very precious. One after the other match blew out in the wind. They gathered around and cupped their hands, did all that woodmen do, but the wind blew out one match after the other. The last match was gone and no fire. One of them said, "Do you suppose we could find a match somewhere in our clothing?" So they searched. Nothing in this pocket. Nothing in that one; nothing here. Each one searched, but found nothing.

Finally, in the hem of one of the coats, one of the men felt a little hard thing, not very long. He said, "I wonder . . ." He ripped open the hem with a knife and found a match about a third as long as a match would be, but it had the head on it. He held up this little match head with a third of the match still on it and said, "Do you know the most precious thing in the world?"

"Yes," his traveling partner said, "that match."

"If it holds and catches, we live. If it fails to catch, we die."

They redoubled their efforts, struck it and carefully coaxed the flame to leap up. The ragged edge of a leaf caught and then another and another, then the shavings, then the sticks, then the wood. Soon they had a beautiful fire. The searchers that found them days later found them well because that precious little match head had lit a fire to save them from certain death.

To save you and me from death, everything had been tried. Every kind of sacrifice, every kind of ascetic practice and self-immolation, everything blew out in the moral wind. But there was a man who walked in Galilee and had in His veins only a small amount of blood. The average-sized human being has possibly a gallon and a half of blood. It was not much in the great pool of human blood, but if that did not work, we would have died. But it worked—the blood of Jesus Christ, God's Son, cleanseth from all sin, and for as much as we know, we are redeemed not with silver or gold but with that precious blood of Jesus Christ.

I wonder how many of us know how precious the blood is that we celebrate? But it is only by the preciousness of the blood that any of us are able or worthy to be considered at all by the fine eye of God, and it is only that knowledge that gives me courage to talk about this holy blood. So I do not say, "You should repent"; I say, "We should repent."

If it had failed us, we would have died. But God raised Jesus from the dead, set Him at His own right hand, took that precious blood and sprinkled it on the Judgment Seat, and that Judgment Seat is a Mercy Seat now.

4

THE CHRISTIAN'S HOPE VERSUS ALL OTHER HOPE

But with the precious blood of Christ, as of a lamb without blemish and without spot: Who verily was foreordained before the foundation of the world, but was manifest in these last times for you.

1 PETER 1:19-20

These verses of 1 Peter are a gem, let down like Peter's sheet, right out of heaven, and would be just as applicable to any group of Christians anywhere in the world as they are to this group to whom Peter writes. It would fit into the eternal needs of a church in Korea or among the Zulus or the Indians of South America or the Jews or Gentiles the world over, because it is not timely truth, it is timeless truth. It speaks only of three persons: God, Christ and us.

As a Protestant in a free America, I am at liberty to discuss any topic I might find myself capable of discussing. I might discuss art, for example. I could bone up on that at the library and talk at length about art, or maybe literature. I like to talk about John Milton because I enjoyed him so much in my younger years. I could not talk about music. I might give my ill-informed opinions on politics and world events; and I suppose if I was careful and you were very patient, some benefit might come to us by my so doing.

However, I do not mind telling you now, I find myself smitten with something I think is nothing less than a divine stroke. Eternity is increasingly before my eyes while I pray, and even while I think on religious subjects. I am seized upon by a thought that has become an oppressive thought. It is that the earth is growing old and the judgment is drawing near, and just a wink of God's eye will clear the earth of everyone now living on it.

Everyone imagines himself to be vastly important in the cosmic scheme. But a wink of God's eye only, a flick of God's lash, and everyone now living—the most important and the anonymous and unheard of altogether—shall go the way of the earth. Not one thing of these now so important things will matter. All who live on the earth now will stand very shortly in awful silence and see the record of their lives exhibited before them. All distinctions—race, color, money or social level—will disappear.

God will not see our diplomas, our bank accounts or the color of our skin, but He will look at us as human beings only—beings made in the image of God, having sinned, then having been redeemed and that redemption made available to us; but whether we are saved or not will lie with us.

This hope of redemption is always upon me as a background of everything I say, conditioning and determining the tone as well as the choice of my material.

Our Foreordained Savior

Peter says that Christ, the Lamb, was foreordained before the foundation of the world. That "foundation of the world" expression can either mean the bringing into being of created things or the ordering of the vast wild forces into an ordered universe. Or it can mean both. Sometimes it means one or the other, depending on the context. Sometimes it means both; sometimes you do not know which it means.

But before God brought into being time and space and matter and law to make what we call the world, Jesus Christ was foreknown and foreordained. In the beginning, God took the vast wild forces that move through His worlds and ordered them into a universe. As though a watchmaker were to take pieces of a watch scattered all over the top of the table and through his knowledge and skill so arrange them that they now, all compact and beautiful in a case, tell the time of day to the split second, so God took all these vast forces and this illimitable matter He had formed and within the framework of space and time ordered it into the world. Before this, Christ was our foreordained Savior.

God did not rush in to apply first aid when man sinned. Sometimes in our instinct for a direct statement, we forget and allow the impression that when man sinned, God looked around for a remedy. This is not the case. Before man sinned, the remedy had already been provided. Before paradise was lost, paradise had already been regained. Because Christ was crucified before the foundation of the world and in the mind and purpose of God, Christ had already died before He was born. In the purpose of God, Christ had already died before Adam was created. In the purpose and plan of God, the world had already been redeemed before the world was ever brought into being. Paradise lost did not drive God to some distracted action and bring about redemption, but paradise lost was foreseen before the world was and before paradise existed. God had already preordained and foreknown the Lamb that was without spot or blemish, and this purpose in eternity lay in the mind of God.

The Spaceless, Timeless One in Space and Time

This foreordained event was manifest in time. It was predetermined before time, but was manifest in time. That is, man sinned in time and space, and therefore, the Timeless One came to time and space in order that He might undo that which was done in space and time by a man, one who was pure in spirit. Because there were creatures who had sinned in the flesh, He Himself became flesh in order that He might put to death that which was destroying the human race. So the Spaceless One came to space, and the Timeless One came to time; and He who is pure spirit above matter took upon Himself a material body and came so that man's sinning, done in a material body, could be redeemed by Jesus Christ in a material body.

That sounds as though it might be simply a repetition of truth already known. If we ever lose the ability to wonder about this, we are in grave need of soul searching and spiritual revival. If we ever lose the wonder out of our hearts, just to hear these words, "Christ, foreknown before the foundation of the world but manifest in time for you," if those words ever cease to move your heart, then your heart is hard.

Saint Bernard of Clairvaux was a godly saint and teacher in medieval France. He had a pupil under him that he thought a great deal of, and taught him, prayed for him and helped him along. The pupil who outstripped his teacher became Pope Eugenius III.

Clairvaux wrote him a letter and said, "You may be Pope, but don't think that that affects me. Love does not know office and love can never be put in awe by any man's position. The reason I am writing you this is, when I knew you, you had a warm heart and served God. Now, you have a big job, everybody is around you, and you have a lot to do. What I am afraid of is that your heart will get hard. If you want to know what a hard heart is, don't ask me, ask Pharaoh, he knows. The very fact you think you don't have a hard heart is plenty evidence that you have it already."

I would thank any man for reminding me that it is entirely possible for a man who in early days walked humbly with others to develop a hard heart because of elevated position. This old saint of God saw what was happening and warned his young pupil. If these old-fashioned simple conventional statements of scriptural truth do not move you or in some degree affect you inwardly when you hear them, then it is time for you to carefully rethink your condition and search your own heart to see if perhaps that has already taken place. That hardness of heart, which Bernard of Clairvaux spoke of, may have already happened to you and greatly needs your attention if you are flippantly sure that it has not taken place.

I like those two little words "for you" in 1 Peter 1:20. What was the purpose of it all? Well, it was "for you." Why was He born? It was "for you." Why did He die? "For you." Why did He arise? "For you." Why is He at the right hand of God? "For you." And for whom is He now making intercession? It is "for you."

In public service, I try to be dignified and not embarrass people with intimacies, but when I am with God by myself, I have no hesitation at all in becoming just as intimate as my faith will allow. When we come to the words "for you," I do not hesitate to write that right in my Bible. I go over some of my old Bibles that have become so badly worn that I had to retire them and I find some things that almost embarrass me now with the simplicity of them and the intimacy of them that I put myself in there.

I will never forget the first prayer I made in public. I attended a church supper, and they asked me to pray. I had never prayed in public before so I stood up and said, "Lord, bless the missionaries, Amen." That was my first public prayer. I suppose a great many people pray as general as that prayer. I did not tell God what missionaries nor did I request anything in particular. I was just getting out of a jam. It is possible to think about redemption as being so general that there is nothing particular about it. I repeat, you can get so general that nobody gets any good out of anything.

"You" is a pronoun, of course, standing in place of a noun, and that noun is you. If you just put your name in there, it will

mean you. So all this preordination, all this before-time pur-
posing of God, this coming of the spotless Lamb into the world
and shedding of His most precious blood, it was all done specifically "for you." Not that it was done also for the whole world,
but it was done for you. A thing can be for the whole world and
nobody can benefit from it. So while we believe in the univer-
sal atonement of His blood, we also believe in a specific atonement, which means you and me. Our name, our number, our
size. We, ourselves, can be identified that it is done for us.

In 1 Peter 1:21 it says, "Who by him do believe in God."
There can be no true believing in God apart from Christ. Out
in the world a great many people believe in God. You can see it
in the newspapers, the Saturday magazines and in many of our
bestseller books. A number of religious books have become
bestsellers and are sold in drugstores. The publishers are saying
a wonderful new something is taking place. People are interested in religion. One magazine had an essay that the world
could be saved by religion and gave the various religions, and
Christianity was one of them.

If the Bible is God's book, and Peter was God's apostle, and
this New Testament is divinely inspired, then I am led to conclude that real belief in God can come only through Christ. Any
other kind of faith in God or belief about God is spotty, imperfect, perverted and very often erroneous. Some things we can
know about God with certainty. We can know His eternal power
and Godhead. The American Indian standing on the shore of
the lake raises his arms to the Great Spirit, evoking the help of
the Great Spirit on his hunting trip. That was an approach to
God of some sort and was some kind of belief. Thomas Edison

is reputed to say that he believed God was force, and if he could live long enough he believed he could invent an instrument sensitive enough to detect God. That was some kind of belief in God.

The deists, such as Voltaire and others, thought of God as a great principal, but He was not a great personality. That was some kind of belief in God. And the heathen in their blindness have some kind of belief in God. In the end, any belief in God is better than no belief in God. That is open to question, but at least for the moment, I give you my tentative statement that it is better to believe in God in a vague, shadowy way than not to believe there is a God.

From Him, Through Him, and to Him Are All Things

But how much better to say, "You who through Him do believe in God." You believe in God not as a pagan, not as an American Indian on the shore of the lake, not as a Yogi looking at his nose and controlling his bodily forces. You believe in God as the one who raised Christ from the dead and gave Him glory. You will find what that means in John 17:24: "Father," said Jesus, "I will that they whom thou hast given me, be with me where I am; that they may behold my glory, which thou hast given me: for thou lovedst me before the foundation of the world." The glory, which God had given Him before the foundation of the world, God restored to Him when He raised Him from the dead.

Then Peter says, "that your faith and hope might be in God" (v. 21). Hope is a beautiful word but it is also a treacherous thing because it is possible to indulge an invalid hope that has no foundation. For instance, a condemned man scheduled to die next Friday, one minute after midnight, never ceases to hope. He believes to the very last that his sentence will be commuted or he will be pardoned. With every knock on his cell door, his eyes brighten with the hope that this means the Governor has stayed the sentence or at least taken the sting of death out of it. But the condemned man is going to die, convinced to the end that he could not die, indulging in a hope that failed him. The condemned man's hope is a treacherous hope.

Many a mother hopes through to the end that her boy will return when all the time her boy is lying on the battlefield, his physical body gone back into decay in some far hidden corner of some burnt-over battlefield. The hope that she would see her boy failed her; it was a treacherous hope, without foundation.

I can hardly go on here without remembering Alfred, Lord Tennyson's famous and touching illustration of the young woman who expected her sailor lover back from the sea. She knew just when he was supposed to arrive at her cottage and dressed for that occasion. Tennyson tells in tender cheer of how she stood before the mirror, turned every way and did the last little touch that she knew he loved. Tennyson wrote, "Poor girl she doesn't know that already his lifeless body is being tossed and heaved on the billows following the wreck."

Hope may be a deceitful and treacherous thing, but real faith never disappoints because it is in God, grounded on the character of God, the promises of God, the covenant of God and the oath of God.

A promise, even an oath before the judicial courts, is only worth the character of the one who makes it. Character has to be there before there can be promise and oath and covenant, and the Scriptures say this Jesus Christ the Lamb led us to a faith in God so that our hope might be in God.

If God is God, then our hope is sound. And we Christians can walk around absolutely sure that everything is all right because we have God back of us: His oath, His covenant, His blood to support us in the whelming flood. Because God could not swear by any other, He swore by Himself.

The Solid Rock
His oath, His covenant, His blood,
Support me in the whelming flood.
When all around my soul gives way,
He then is all my hope and stay.
On Christ the solid rock I stand,
All other ground is sinking sand.
—Edward Mote (1797-1874)

5

THE FUNDAMENTAL DIFFERENCE BETWEEN THE CHRISTIAN AND THE NON-CHRISTIAN

Seeing ye have purified your souls in obeying the truth through the Spirit unto unfeigned love of the brethren, see that ye love one another with a pure heart fervently.

1 PETER 1:22

The more familiar I become with the Scriptures, the more I am pleased with the logic of the Bible. It moves along with beautiful precision and marches like an army, expecting you to move with it by the Holy Ghost. At times it will take liberty of a digression. Paul is full of them. The scholars call Paul's style elliptical. He starts to say one thing and then he will look over, see something else, lose the thread of his thought and dash over and say something better. He leaves the statement of his intention to be inferred from his preceding words.

Peter does the same thing here in 1 Peter 1:22. In the Bible, wherever there is a complete statement, the thought always follows beautiful logic. "Now seeing that ye have done this one thing" or "seeing that this one thing is true of you, therefore, see if something else is true of you."

The Bible never breaks in to your heart with a command, but always precedes it with a reason for it. The New Testament always gives biblical reasons for what it demands. There is never anything whimsical about the Holy Ghost. There is imperious command, but it always grows out of some sound, logical reason why it is perfectly natural and right and why it should be solved. So he says, "Seeing that you have purified your heart . . . therefore, love."

Most of the great religions of the world begin with the externals. In fact, I am unable to think of any that does not begin with the external. The starting point is usually with diet, dress, ascetic practices or the celebration of days. Then the hope is that somehow by the performance of external acts they will be able to work in on themselves to the heart. By beginning with the fingers, they hope to work through to the heart. Beginning with the toes, they can work up to the heart. Those are the religions of the world.

It would be amusing, if it were not too significant of a trend, to see how such groups as Hollywood actors and night-club performers and all the rest are going in big for Yoga these days. Everybody wants to be Yogi. The Yogi, of course, is one that begins outside and by certain body practices and postures, controls his breathing. After getting his breathing under control, he controls his thoughts and slowly works it in to his inner man. The hope is that he will change himself and purify his soul by something he does on the outside.

That is exactly contrary to the Scriptures. To begin on the outside and then work into the center is unknown to the New Testament. This was the difference between our Lord Jesus Christ and the Pharisees. The Pharisees were concerned about the exterior, while Jesus majored on the internal. The Pharisees thought that by practicing external things they could change their internal. Jesus knew better and challenged this position throughout His ministry. He taught that it was the heart that mattered. The internal matters, and when the internal is right, the outside will fall into line perfectly. This is also the difference between modernistic doctrines and liberalistic religions. They begin by training and making much of religious education.

Religious education at best is training men and women to think right and act right. Certainly, it is not to be decried, but rather desired. But without the secret and mysterious internal change, all of this outside change ultimately will be found only wasted.

I conclude from my study of the Bible that the faith of Christ begins in the center, the heart and mind, and works out to the external conduct. I am safe in concluding that if the heart has not been reached, all religious profession is completely vain. If the heart has been reached, religious profession then takes on meaning. Does it sound like an old bromide or religious cliché for me to repeat? What you hear so much from the average evangelist, and he's right in it, is that you can join all the churches in the city, be baptized by every mode known and celebrate every holy day in the Christian calendar and still be lost if you are not changed on the inside.

The soul is inside of the person, the essence of the person, that which matters. The word "soul" here certainly can be and is intended to mean the whole interior man. Synonyms for "soul" would be the "heart" of the man or the "reins" of the man, but it is the whole interior man, and it is this man that has been purified. There is a purification of the deep inner life that is required before we have any right to believe that our religious profession is valid. Now, the question is, How is the inner man purified?

The Truth About Purification

The Hindus practice purification of the soul by bathing in the River Ganges; but the catch is, all they ever get is external bathing. Those that have seen the mother Ganges say that it is not much, because mother Ganges is too dirty to cleanse anybody. We do not smile at them nor look down our holy noses at them, for the simple reason that they are trying to do a right thing. They are seeking right in the wrong way, and they will never reach it, just as a man might start to drive to Detroit but mistakenly turn his car in the direction of Omaha. He might be ever so honest in his mistaken direction, and some may smile quietly inside, remembering the time they did that very thing.

A truck driver told of an incident that happened to him. The scheme was that two men worked the same truck. There was a bunk where one would sleep while the other drove. That way they would always have a fresh driver. This truck driver was driving once while his co-driver was sleeping in the little bunk back of the driver. He drove going east, saw a filling station, swung completely around, made a U-turn and parked. He filled the truck with diesel fuel, woke his friend and said, "It's your turn. Time for you to drive for a while." He climbed in the bunk and went sound asleep. Twenty-five miles later, the new driver discovered his friend had turned the truck around.

He was perfectly honest in his efforts, but completely erroneous. His driving direction was a mistake. He had 50 miles to make up because of an error.

You might say, "But he is such a good man." It does not make any difference; he was going the wrong way.

"But he pays his debts and he just loves his wife." It does not make any difference; he was traveling the wrong way and he will never get to the terminal if he continues going the wrong direction.

"But he is so handsome, and a man with hair like that could not make a mistake." He did make the mistake, nevertheless.

"But he belongs to the mission society and he is a church member." But he was going the wrong way. And no matter who is going the wrong way, or how nice he is, or how bushy his hair, if he is going the wrong way, his personality will not get him going the right way.

For thousands of people the devil has turned their vehicle around and they do not know it. They are pushing the pedal right down to the floor and are going along beautifully, imagining that they are going where they want to go because they are making good progress. But they are not going the right direction. The Yogi who gets his breathing under control and can properly manipulate his abdominal muscles, who can hypnotize himself and draw in his thoughts, is making progress all right, but he is traveling the wrong direction. He is assuming the validity of an erroneous doctrine that the heart is made pure beginning from without. Whereas Scripture says the heart is made pure first and everything else comes after it.

How do we purify our heart? By obeying the truth.

Obedience Purifies Faith

Do not be shocked by that word "obey." It is not popular today, but it is a good word: obeying the truth.

There are two sides to purification: obeying and believing. Acts 15:9 says, "[God] purifying their hearts by faith." And in our text Peter says, "Seeing ye have purified your souls in obeying the truth." Therefore, we have faith and works. One truth is from Peter's text, and the other is from the Holy Spirit in the book of Acts. Here is where our critics come along and point out a seeming contradiction. But there is no contradiction whatsoever.

I can illustrate this by looking at the seagull. Suppose I was making a big deal over the seagull's beautiful right wing, and I said, "The seagull has one of the most graceful right wings you ever saw. Watch him as he extends that right wing, pushes it up and out, and shakes it, and it is so graceful." An artist would run for his pencil and outline the symmetry and beauty of that wing. From that, we teach the validity of flight by the right wing of the seagull.

Soon somebody comes along and says, "Have you ever noticed the left wing of the seagull? It is simply beautiful." The first man says, "You are a heretic and a legalist that you would dare mention that the seagull has a left wing. Why, our whole church is built on the doctrine of the right wing." The critic stands off and says, "Listen to that argument; they're contradicting each other."

You Can't Have One Without the Other

The claim of contradiction is foolish, for everyone knows a seagull cannot fly with one wing. He would only flap in a circle and never get off the ground. There is not a seagull anywhere in the world that could fly with only one wing. He would fly in a circle and spin the other direction. If he tried to fly with his right wing, he would go counter-clockwise; if he tried to fly with his left wing he would go clockwise, but he would be where he started after he was finished flapping.

This is the trouble in our churches today. Just as soon as you join the church, you are given five jobs and become chair of a committee and away you go. People wear themselves out flapping their left wing. But talk to them about a new birth, about a cleansing on the inside, about a renewal of the soul and they do not know what you mean. "Our crowd specializes on left wings and we do not believe much in activity; we just believe in believing." But if you will believe the Bible instead of believing half-truth and see that when one man says, "You are purified by faith," and another man says, "You are purified by obeying," they are not contradicting, but simply giving you both wings of the bird. Faith has to have works or it flaps in a circle. And works have to have faith or the works are dead. So by works and faith we go along.

The eleventh chapter of the book of Hebrews is called the "faith chapter," but have you ever noticed that it is also a works chapter? "By faith Abel offered unto God a more excellent sacrifice than Cain" (Heb. 11:4). He offered it by faith, but he did offer it in obedience to some revelation God had given him. "By faith Enoch was translated" (v. 5), but also Enoch, by works, walked with God until he was no longer. "By faith Noah . . . prepared an ark" (v. 7), and by works he prepared an ark.

It took work to build the ark. If Noah had set down on a wooden horse, piled his clothes beside him and said, "I'm just believing," he would never have built the ark. But he called in his carpenters, laid down his blueprints and went to work.

Somebody came along and said, "You hope to save yourself by building an ark? You are not a New Testament Christian; you are a legalist; you are mixing works with faith."

"No," Noah might have replied, "I'm obeying my faith by doing what I'm told." Therefore, Noah built himself an ark.

Go down the line in the faith chapter, Hebrews 11, until you come to Abraham. "By faith Abraham . . . went out" (v. 8), but he went out by faith. Gideon did things by faith, but he also did them by works. He actually girded on his sword and went out. Then there was Barrack and Samson. Samson could have sat idle and gazed at the heavens and said, "I am believing," and the Philistines would have swarmed around him. But he grabbed the jawbone of an ass and slew about a thousand Philistines. Then there was Jetha, David and Samuel, and on down the line. Hebrews 11 is not only a faith chapter, but it is also a works chapter. God never makes a whole chapter of one wing. He puts in the other wing even if it is not readily visible.

Someone may say, "That is teaching the power of the human character to do good." No, it is not, because Peter said, "through the Spirit." God never commands righteousness without giving power to be righteous. So it is through the Holy Ghost. The real Christian who has been renewed inside and purified in his soul has no confidence in the flesh. He knows the flesh will never get him anywhere. He knows that the works of the law might be fulfilled in us who walk in the Spirit and not in the flesh.

True Love

Peter goes on to say, "unto unfeigned love of the brethren." What does this all lead to?

That word "unfeigned" is an interesting word. Unregenerate society mostly feigns its love. Politicians feign their love; they will kiss your baby and even kiss your hand. They smile, they visit, they travel around, make whistle stops, wave the flag, quote Lincoln, and all to get your vote. They love you so much. When they make their speeches, they refer to you in drooling affection because you have the sovereign power to put an X after their name on the voting ballot.

I often think how some of these lugubrious tears that union leaders shed over the poor, exploited and downtrodden are crocodile tears because the leaders call people in, call them out, make fools out of them and treat them like puppets while they ride around in brand-new Cadillacs.

Unions are a good thing if they are carefully run. I have always believed that. I also believe that they can become curses when in the hands of men who only claim to love the public but in reality love their pocketbook and their own power.

Then there is the salesman. A salesman comes to your door after finding out your name next door, and it is "Mrs. Jones, how nice to see you." He found out next door who you are and enquired about your family. "Did Jim get back from the war yet?" he asks, but only because he wants to sell you something.

The unregenerate world feigns its love for the most part, except for its own tiny circle. But the Spirit implants in us real love. Unfeigned love of the brethren and the love of a Christian are not a feigned love.

I remember years ago visiting a church. I just sat in the back and looked straight ahead, waiting for the service to begin. Soon the pastor came around and fawned over me. You would have thought I was Eisenhower's long-lost twin brother. He did not know who I was. He said, "I'm so glad you decided to look in on us." I had not; I had only gone to church. I did not quite accept that; it was a little too much. When you love me too much, I am worried about you. Love me enough and it is all right. Do not love me at all and I will pray for you. When it gets to be fawning love, it is feigned love.

The Holy Ghost gives us love that is real. Real love does not always fawn over its object. Real love sometimes rebukes. The sharpest book in the New Testament is the epistle of First John. The apostle of love also could exercise the paddle more vigorously than any other apostle. So the loving John could lay it on when necessary. The Scripture says, "For whom the LORD loveth he correcteth; even as a father the son in whom he delighteth" (Prov. 3:12).

"See now that ye love one another" (1 Pet. 1:22). Obviously, this love is not a wild plant that will grow of itself. It is there in the heart by a divine planting, but it must be cultivated. Dandelions will grow without cultivation, but love must be cultivated. The human heart must be cultivated; we must work on it. We must pray, search the Word, obey, believe and humble ourselves, opening our minds to the incoming Holy Ghost so that we might cultivate and see that we love one another.

How? "With a pure heart." No other kind of heart can love purely; because for the heart to love purely it must love unselfishly. Unselfish love does not exploit its object and it does not ask anything in return. That is so lofty that the modern world knows little or nothing about it. But it is out of a pure heart.

This true love is to be demonstrated "fervently." God hates everything that is halfway. He hates half-minded people: "Ye are double minded," He said. A double mind is half one way and half the other. "A double minded man is unstable in all his ways" (Jas. 1:8). God hates the double mind and says, "He that wavereth is like a wave of the sea driven with the wind and tossed . . . let not that man think that he shall receive any thing of the Lord" (vv. 6-7). Have some kind of mind. Settle for one mind, but let it be all one thing. Do not let it be a divided mind, for that is what a double mind is.

Out in the country, some people were called Sunday Christians. Their religion was only a Sunday affair, and people would poke fun at them and say they hung their religion up with their new suit in the closet when they got home on Sunday night and never put it on again until the next Sunday morning. That is being double-minded. God hates all double-mindedness because

73

it is not real. He said we are to love fervently out of a pure heart. Fervent love, fiery love, fevered love. God says, "Ephraim, he hath mixed himself among the people; Ephraim is a cake not turned" (Hos. 7:8).

I was brought up on buckwheat cakes, and I know what a half-turned cake is. It is fully baked only on one side. The Lord hates half-baked things. He wants it to be baked all the way through.

Then Peter talks about being lukewarm. Is a bottle half full of something, or half empty? Is lukewarm water half warm or half cold? Is a half Christian a half sinner and half Christian? I do not know, but I do know this: God will sweep the whole business out together. He will have nothing to do with half stuff. Did He say that we are to be full unto the half fullness of God? Never. For God to say a thing like that, He would not be God. Filled unto the fullness of God, He said, not unto the half fullness. God has nothing to do with half-full things. He gives us a whole day, not a half day; He gives us a whole personality, not a half personality; a whole mind, not a half mind; a whole salvation, not a half salvation. And He expects our love to be a whole love, fervent and not half cold. "So then because thou art lukewarm, and neither cold nor hot, I will spue thee out of my mouth" (Rev. 3:16).

Think it over. See that you have purified your soul by believing the truth through the Spirit unto one thing, love of the brethren. See to it that love goes to work and you really do love each other fervently out of a pure heart.

6

THE CHRISTIAN PUTS ASIDE CERTAIN THINGS

Wherefore laying aside all malice, and all guile, and hypocrisies, and envies, and all evil speakings, as newborn babes, desire the sincere milk of the word, that ye may grow thereby: If so be ye have tasted that the Lord is gracious.

1 PETER 2:1-3

Many words are little more than fillers. They are conjunctives, even though grammarians would not call them so. They just connect; "therefore" and "wherefore" and such words are among them. But when the Holy Spirit uses "wherefore" or "therefore" or "whereas," we must always look at what comes before, because "wherefore" means because of what is said before.

"Wherefore laying aside all malice . . . as newborn babes, desire the sincere milk of the word." We have the connection there if you pay some attention to the word "as." Peter says that we are

75

born again—a biological term that has to do with birth and life and organisms. It is not a poetical term, nor a legal one; it is a biological term. Peter was a follower of our Savior and possibly present when He said in that great third chapter of John, "Except a man be born again, he cannot see the kingdom of God" (v. 3). Peter remembered that and repeated, "Being born again, not of corruptible seed, but of incorruptible, by the word of God" (1 Pet. 1:23). He says here, "not of corruptible seed, but of incorruptible, by the word of God, which liveth and abideth for ever" (v. 24). This heavenly birth is contrasted with all earthly births.

There was a science—if you want to call it a science, a subhead under science at least—called "eugenics." A great exponent of eugenics was Albert E. Wiggim, who wrote, when he was a younger and more vigorous man, a good deal on the subject. Eugenics simply means that we apply to humanity the same system we apply to the barnyard. If a farmer wants good stock, he breeds from increasingly select parents, and this was the science of eugenics.

For a while, eugenics went very strong, but then died out. Adolph Hitler took it seriously and believed in the super race. He even went so far as to say that certain, select men should be picked out of the populace and made the fathers of all the generations, and thus you would increase your stock, raise its level, by breeding from good high stock. That is well known to farmers, but Hitler applied it to humanity.

The science of eugenics, though not quite so crass as that, nevertheless taught that we should pick out only those fathers and mothers from the general populace that had such health and such a fine face as we would want to breed into the generations to come. Of course, that meant that anyone who had anything "wrong" with his appearance or health would remain childless by law. So that is eugenics.

But even granted that such a thing might happen . . . if everyone under six foot should legally be declared as a celibate and get married, and every young woman that had anything wrong with her eyes or anything wrong with her at all would be compelled to remain childless, and all future Americans should be great stalwart fellows, two things would be true of those super babies: They would be corrupt and finally die. "Corruption" and "mortality" are two words the devil put in this world, and you can never get them out. You can breed a race of giants, but after they have run their course, they all will die, they all will rot.

The Holy Ghost here contrasts the birth from above with any birth from below. And He says, "Being born again, not of corruptible seed, but of incorruptible, by the word of God, which liveth and abideth for ever. For all flesh is as grass, and all the glory of man [even the glory of the eugenic man] as the flower of grass. The grass withereth, and the flower thereof falleth away: but the word of the Lord endureth for ever" (1 Pet. 1:23-25). It takes God to put everlastingness into anything. It takes God to shoot the basic element of eternity into anything, and if God does not do it, the two curse words rest upon it, "mortality" and "corruptibility."

Whether a race be plain people like us, or whether they might be some superior race of supermen dreamed by Nietzsche or Hitler or Wiggim, it will die sometime, for it is written, "It is appointed unto men once to die, but after this the judgment" (Heb. 9:27). The richest parents in this world today, the best educated and those with the highest IQ may hold in their arms a baby that may have a wonderful future, with fine health and intelligence, and it may have all the opportunities for intellectual and cultural improvement. But God Almighty has said, "The soul that sinneth, it shall die" (Ezek. 18:4).

The most cultured and healthy parents cannot take the word "die" out of their baby's heart. Love it, weep on it and baptize it with their tears all they will, they cannot take the word "mortality" out of their baby's life, for mortality and corruption remain. They follow, like some dark shadow, every human being. These twin clouds, mortality and corruption, rest about the perfumed boudoir of every Hollywood actress. They rest like twin clouds of doom above the chair of the White House where sits our president. And wherever men are found, if we could only see, we would see these two weeping clouds above them—mortality and corruption. "Mortality" and "corruption" are beautiful words; but when we throw the Anglo-Saxon at them and say "die" and "rot," these are not so beautiful.

Incorruptible Words

Latin words always have a way of rumbling along like a music wagon and say some beautiful things that are terrible things nonetheless, but the blunt Anglo-Saxon always pulls it down where it belongs. So men die and rot, and the Holy Ghost contrasts the birth that dies and rots with the birth that is incorruptible and never dies. Thank God! "Being born again, not of corruptible seed, but of incorruptible, by the word of God, which liveth and abideth for ever." That is the word of the gospel that is preached unto you.

Because this is true, we lay aside all wickedness—that is what the word "malice" means here, wickedness. I have studied this very carefully and have examined the words, searched them and prayed in order that I might get truth. And I have examined Peter's words "laying aside" in this verse. What did Peter really say? His use of the words "laying aside" could mean one of two things: either "taking off and changing," as you would do with a garment, or "cleansing away defilement," as you might wash a garment.

So, what he said was, put away from you either by "taking it off and throwing it from you" or by "purging yourself from all malice." It is something you and I can do. Spineless Christianity says there is nothing to do, but the Word of God does not go along with that. If you read your Bible, you will be sharp enough to read what God says about these taken-for-granted subjects. "*You* lay aside"; *you* are the subject of the sentence. You are the one who activates the verb. You are the person who does it. You are the subject of the sentence. He says that it is something we can do.

Someone may say, "Mr. Tozer, how can a man cleanse his own heart? How can a man purge his own soul?" I might ask you how can a man wash his own hands? He cannot; he can only subject his hands to water and detergents and they do the washing. If he does not subject himself to water and detergent, he will not be cleansed. Just as a man is clean by washing his hands and yet cannot wash his hands, so a man's heart is cleansed when he cleanses himself, and yet he cannot cleanse himself.

No contradiction here, simply a question of understanding. When you say to your son, "Johnny, wash your hands before you sit down to the dinner table," Johnny disappears, and soon he is back holding up white hands. Shortly before, they had not been so white. Now, did Johnny wash his hands? No, and yes. He washed them by bringing them into contact with water and detergent, which did the washing.

God says to a sinner, "Cleanse your hands, ye sinners; and purify your hearts, ye double-minded" (Jas. 4:8). What does He mean? Before you sit down at the Father's table, go wash your hands, and yet that sinner cannot wash his hands. Not all the water in the world can wash him clean, only the blood of Christ can do it. Why then is he told to do it? For the same reason the boy is told to go wash. There is water that will cleanse him, but if he does not use water and soap, his hands will still be dirty, and when he rubs them, he only rubs in the dirt.

So when we who are religious hear the voice of God telling us to lay aside all impurities, we rush to lay them aside and do not go where the blood is or the cleansing. Only the blood of Jesus Christ can cleanse us, yet if we hold ourselves from that blood, we will be unclean forever.

Lay Aside All Impurity

Here is what he says we must cleanse ourselves from, or put away as dirty clothing: We must put away from ourselves all wickedness. Wickedness means all vice, and vice means whatever is not of virtue. Right here, the liberals hurt themselves.

At times when I talk to students, I shake my head and turn away and feel like saying, "Go from the presence of a foolish man, when thou perceivest not in him the lips of knowledge" (Prov. 14:7). Instead of turning from all wickedness, they ask the question, "What is wickedness?" or "What is virtue?" A sincere Christian should never ask any hypothetical questions.

A boy, hungry as two bears, makes a beeline for the table and is told, "Johnny, you can't eat like that; go wash." How would you like it if he stopped and said, "Mother, would you please define dirt and what you mean by it?" You would soon drive him off to the bathroom, wouldn't you? Yet we treat God like that. God said, "Get rid of all your defilement," and yet we write books to show what defilement is and write chapters showing what virtue is, and when it's all over we are just where we were before.

Socrates, the blunt-nosed philosopher of Athens centuries ago, had quite a sense of humor as well as a very profound mind; and he used to gather many young fellows around him and take a walk. One of those young men was Plato. It would be well worth your while to sit down and read some of those long dialogues of Plato. They are the words and the doings of Socrates.

One had to do with friendship. They walked and talked, walked, sat and got up, talked and walked some more, and all the time they were walking they were talking, and what do you suppose they were talking about? They were talking about friendship and inquiring what friendship is. Somebody would suggest that friendship was this and another would say it was something else. Then Socrates would quietly go to work and devastate that argument and show that that was not friendship at all. And when it was all over and they were dead tired and hungry, they still had not arrived at any conclusion. Socrates laughed and said to the young students around him, "It's astonishing isn't it, how good friends we are and yet we don't know what friendship is." They were all his good friends and not a one of them knew the definition of friendship.

It is entirely possible for a man to put away all vice and dedicate his life to the cultivation of holy virtue and not know what vice and virtue is philosophically. You do not have to know. Every born-again Christian knows virtue and vice by the light of conscience and the clear light of the Scriptures. The light of conscience, if it has not been degraded by miseducation, could tell us what is vice and what is virtue; and if we subject our conscience to the searching discipline of the Scriptures, we will know. We will know what is right for us and what is wrong for us without knowing what the definition of right or wrong is philosophically.

I might add along with Socrates that it is wonderful how holy a man may get without knowing what holiness is. So it is said, "Put away all vice." Do not argue about it, just put it away.

Put Away All Guile

Then Peter says to put away all guile. The word "guile" comes from a hunter catching a bird with bait. But let's take the example of a mouse.

Every mouse thinks for a few terrible seconds that the housewife loves him because he is a great lover of cheese and the housewife sets a feast of cheese before him. If two philosophical mice were to be seen scrambling across the kitchen on their way somewhere, discussing how they were in bad with the housewife, and then when they saw this huge succulent feast of odoriferous cheese waiting for them there, they might look at each other and say, "We've wronged her, she really remembers us, God bless her. She put out a little meal for us." And if one of them were as wise as he should be, he would say, "Watch that cheese, I know that lady, and she put before you not a meal but bait. This isn't food, this is bait." The headstrong mouse says, "I have misjudged the whole human race. Why this was set for me." Snap! And it is all over with that mouse. The next day, he is picked up, one more victim of his own credulity.

"Guile" is the scriptural word for "mouse bait"—"put away all guile." In other words, do not put one thing for another to fool anybody. But be exactly what you are. Is that not wonderful? So practical that it is salty good sense.

The Pharisees were the most guileful of all people in history inasmuch as they would ask a question of Jesus and then follow it with another question, all the time hiding bait underneath in order that they might trap something that came out of His mouth. Jesus used their very words to catch them. They were setting bait before the Savior, but He never fell into it.

The Christian ought never to say one thing to mean another. And he ought not to mean another thing when he says one thing; and he never should two-time or double-talk, but always be just what he is and mean what he says.

The Quakers reacted violently from the careless speech of their day among Christians, and they carried it so far that they would not even use the word Mr. or Mrs., Master or Mistress. They said, "We don't know if he's a Master, we'll just call him John." Because Quakers did not believe in giving any titles that might mislead, they would not even say "you" because that was plural; they said "thee" and "thou" rather than "you," because "he" is not two people; "he" is one.

83

That was carrying it too far, which amounted to bondage to words. We never should get under bondage to words but should mean exactly what we say. It is altogether possible for Christians to get under bondage to language and get under what one man called the "tyranny of words."

Hypocrisy lies close to guile but is not the same. Hypocrisy is to act with another's character, to pretend to be what we are not or pretend not to be what we are. A true Christian never hides anything because a true Christian never needs to hide anything. If there is anything in your life that you need to hide, then you are not living the kind of life you should be living. No Christian, if he is right with God, should ever need to hide anything in his life.

That does not mean I must publish the amount of my income tax or that I must tell all of the embarrassing intimacies that are a part of any human life. That is another matter. It does mean, as far as moral conduct is concerned, that there is nothing to hide. Do not be a hypocrite, but be exactly what you are. Do not pretend to be what you are not, and do not pretend not to be what you are.

Put Away All Envying

I looked up the word "envy" in one of the best commentaries in the world; just a good old-fashioned dictionary. I came to the word "envies" here and wondered what Noah Webster said about it. Here is what Webster said. It may make some of us squirm, but here is what he said, "envy, chagrin, mortification, discontent or uneasiness at the sight of someone else's excellence or good fortune." It is when you see somebody else having excellencies or good fortune, and the effect upon you is to make you uneasy or discontented, mortified or chagrined. Now that is envy.

It might be that someone is asked to play a solo in church service, and another soloist sees him and immediately feels rising within him chagrin, discontent and uneasiness. One man gets a call to a big church and the other members of the conference feel within them chagrin, discontent and uneasiness. One man gets a long car and another man feels within him chagrin, mortification and uneasiness, and so on through all the ramifications of human life. Envy is to feel uneasy when somebody else is being praised.

I have noticed that envy never crosses a line. One man is a painter, another a pianist; the painter hears the pianist praised without a ripple of unease. He can just join in the praise. He does not mind, because he is a painter, and the pianist is out of his field. But let some other painter be praised in his presence and he is very likely to feel rising in him emotions of discontent, chagrin and uneasiness because the person praised is in his field. You can praise a politician to the sky and it does not bother a singer, but if you praise another singer, he may squirm. It is when somebody in our field of interest is given a place that we are not being given that uneasiness comes.

The Holy Ghost says to put all that away. What do you do with it? What do you do with dirt? You expose it to water and soap. What do you do with the dirt of the heart? You expose it to the blood of the Lamb and the power of the Holy Ghost.

Put Away All Evil Speaking

I often think of how humorously wise the English language is. The word "gossip" is, of course, the evil speaker. A gossip is defined as a defamer, belittler or backbiter. Let us break those words down and kick them around a little bit.

First, the word "defame." Fame, of course is a high reputation somebody has and then along comes somebody and defames him. He just cuts the horns off, dehorns that fame and then we have the word "defame." That is a word almost funny and yet how terrible it is that there are persons who cannot allow another person to be well spoken of in their presence. They will say, "Well, that is true but," and then start to defame the man. So a defamer is somebody that destroys fame.

Next, the word "belittle." That is a fellow who is big, and a fellow comes along and belittles him. Nothing humiliates a person more than to be cut down to size by some bully. Even among Christians, there are those who get tremendous joy of cutting someone down to size. They see somebody trying to do something—perhaps they are a little full of themselves—and they feel obligated to take that big person and try to make them as little as possible. Surely, some people need a little bit of belittling, but woe be unto the person who takes that responsibility on himself.

Then there is the word "backbite." I have always thought that God must have had something to do with creating that word. "Backbite" means to bite behind the back. If you try to bite anybody in front, you have to face their angry eyes and two fists; but it is quite safe to bite from behind, and so we backbite the back.

I am sure that if the envious, the defamers, and the backbiters were taken out of the average church there would be a revival overnight. We backbite, defame, belittle, envy and then piously blame our trouble on the liberals and the modernists. No liberal or modernist troubles the average evangelical church. Both would die because the air is too rare and they could not take it. Bring a modernist into an evangelical church and turn him loose awhile and he would soon hunt for cover because the atmosphere just is not conducive to modernism. He could not live in it. The air is too rare.

We cannot blame the modernists for the state we are in spiritually. We are to blame because we are guilty of guile, hypocrisies, envies, defaming, belittling and backbiting.

Words to Grow By

Peter finishes verse 2 with the words, "Desire the sincere milk of the word, that ye may grow thereby." These sins he has been describing are like children's diseases that retard growth and threaten life. Peter said put them all away and get healthy, and then proceed to live on the sincere milk of the Word. That word "sincere" is a tough one. Peter used a Greek word. We have "sincere" in our *King James Bible,* and the translators have had a tough time with it.

A student and translator ran into this word "sincere" and gave the best explanation I have ever heard. He explained that "sincere" could apply to milk. While he was visiting in Athens, Greece, he noticed coming down the street a milk wagon pulled by a burrow, and on the side of the milk wagon was a sign written in Greek. Being a Greek student, he was able to read it. The sign said, "such and such milk company, we sell only sincere milk." He got it in a second. He knew what it meant. It meant unadulterated milk. No extra water in this milk.

That is what Peter meant when he used that old Greek word. He said, "Feed yourself on the unadulterated Word." Do not water it down. Take it full strength. That is, let the Word of God say to you all it says. Do not simply pick out the happy verses. It would be shocking to go through some Bibles and find how we underline only the happy verses.

Back in old Israel, two groups got up on two different mountains and said "amen" to the reading of the Scriptures. Upon one mountain was one group and upon the other mountain was the other group. The old man of God would read all the blessings and his group would say, "Amen." Then he would read the curses, and up on that other mountain they would say, "Amen." Then he would read some more blessings and the first group would say, "Amen." Then he would read some more curses and the second group would say, "Amen." They took all of God's Word, both the blessings and the curses, both the admonition and the encouragement, both the whippings and the comfort, they took it all.

We must take all the Word of God and not water it down. "Desire the sincere milk of the word, that ye may grow thereby." Our growth is to be by the Word, and it will be the exact proportion to the diet we follow.

Sometimes I have occasion to counsel a backslider. I might say it is a rare case, but when a fellow has slipped and comes to see me, usually he follows the same pattern. He says, "I can't pray anymore; I'm getting careless in the way I'm living; I don't care to go to church much anymore." My one penetrating question usually is, "Do you read the Scriptures?" The answer usually is, "No, not anymore, not as much as I used to."

That is the trouble. The child who does not read the sincere milk of the Word gets weak and run down. If we turn from the Word, we can expect every kind of disease to begin to get hold of us; but the unadulterated Word of God will give us help and make us strong. So we must eat the Word and obey the Word, and then we will grow thereby.

7

CHRISTIANITY: AN EXPERIENCE, NOT AN EXPERIMENT

If so be ye have tasted that the Lord is gracious. To whom coming, as unto a living stone, disallowed indeed of men, but chosen of God, and precious, ye also, as lively stones, are built up a spiritual house, an holy priesthood, to offer up spiritual sacrifices, acceptable to God by Jesus Christ.

1 PETER 2:3-5

One error people make when coming to the Bible is to assume that because a thing is true, it is automatically true of them. That if it is in the Bible, it is true in them. But the assumption is not necessarily so. Peter conditions truth about us on the little word "if" and says, "If ye have tasted them, from what I say from here on is applicable to you; but if you have not tasted, you should go back and taste before you go any further."

The wonder of New Testament Christianity is that "we have tasted the good Word of God and the powers of the world to come. We have tasted that the Lord is gracious."

I want that word "tasted" to mean what it means in the Bible and not what it means when we experiment. Experiment is when we test the thing by putting it to the tongue, as a woman tests her cooking to see if it is salty enough. I suppose that is common, but that is never what the Bible means to test a thing to see if it is all right with no intention of eating it; maybe never going on to eat it at all, but at least knowing what it is like.

This is not what the Bible means. We have only to look up the original meaning to find that the word "taste" here means experience lived through in order that a thing may be real to us and everlastingly ours. It must be experienced; it must be lived through. That same word is used about our Savior in the book of Hebrews. It says, "But we see Jesus, who was made a little lower than the angels for the suffering of death, crowned with glory and honour; that he by the grace of God should taste death for every man" (Heb. 2:9).

Those who teach the tasting doctrine ought to give this some attention. If the word "taste" in the New Testament means tested with the tongue to see if we like it or not, then that is all Jesus did with death. For the same word is used that He tasted death for every man. The word "taste" here does not mean experiment, or to try it by a touch; it means experienced, gone through, encountered, passed into and through, and that is exactly what happed to our Lord when He died on the cross. He did not experiment with death to see whether He liked it; He did not taste it to see whether He dare go on. He threw Himself recklessly out and gave Himself to die, and experienced it in the fullest sense of that word.

The Gift and the Giver
Cannot Be Separated

These believers had experienced not the grace of God only, but that the Lord was gracious. Where there is a difference we ought to note that difference and distinguish things that differ in the language of Paul. He does not say, "If so be that you have tasted of the grace of God," but "If so be ye have tasted that the Lord is gracious." There is difference in testing or tasting, or even experiencing the Word of God or the grace of God and experiencing the gracious God.

We never should separate the gift from the source, the gift from the Giver. We never should say, "I have forgiveness." We should say, "God has forgiven." We never should say, "I have eternal life." We should say, "God has given me eternal life and Christ is my life." The point is, God never separates Himself from His gifts. Whatever God gives, He cannot but give Himself in it. If a man has been forgiven, what has happened to him is that the forgiving God has touched him. God has forgiven him, that is true, but it is God that matters more than the forgiveness. If a man has eternal life, it is that he might know Jesus Christ. That word "know" is "experience" again. We must be careful that we do not separate God's gifts from God Himself.

What is wrong with Christians in our day is that they have the gifts of God but have forgotten the God of the gifts. There is a difference between noble, strong, vigorous and satisfying spiritual experience and the other kind of spiritual experience, which takes the gifts of God but forgets the Giver.

A most ignoble example is found in the Gospels where 10 lepers came to Jesus and were healed of their leprosy and delivered. They were 10 healthy men, and with this new gift of health, they all started away. Nine of them kept right on going, satisfied with the gift of health. But the tenth man happened to remember that he had received a gift from the Giver. His eyes went from the gift to the Giver, and he came back humbly and thanked the Lord Jesus Christ and said sadly, "Where are the nine?" The others were satisfied with the gift, but only one came back to become better acquainted with the Giver.

G. Campbell Morgan once said, "We ought never in our gospel preaching to offer men peace. We ought never in our gospel preaching to offer men repose from their conscience. We ought never to offer them anything short of life." I wholeheartedly agree. We should never divorce any gift we offer to men from the Giver.

In our selfish praying, we come to God with a long grocery list and petition God to do this and this and this and this, and if God answers our prayers, then we cross it off and go on down to the next list and on we go. It just seems to me that this is very saddening to the heart of God to be thus used as a convenience. It seems to me that the Lord Jesus must be very heavy-hearted at times when He finds His redeemed people more taken up with redemption than they are with the Redeemer; when His forgiven people are more taken up with forgiveness than they are with the Forgiver; when His living people to whom He has given life are more taken up with the life than they are with the Life Giver.

We ought to, in our preaching and teaching and personal experience, make a strong return to God Himself, to the person of God. In fact, I am not sure but that we could condense everything we want into sentences beginning with the word "God" or having God in it somewhere. God is, God is present, God loves, God's Word, God's Holy Spirit, God's Messiah. Everything belongs, begins, ends and continues with God.

Four Things That Can Be Said About These Christians

Peter said, "If ye have tasted and experienced that the Lord is gracious, your experience has been with the gracious Lord unto whom is coming." This was true of them as it is true of all real Christians everywhere. I give you four prepositions in Peter's description: They came "out," they came "away," they came "together" and they came "unto." Probably not in that order, and they did not do it together; but they may have come one at a time or two at a time. Taken all together, these four things can be said about these Christians.

First, they came "out" of the world. We try to take the world into the church, sanctify it, baptize it, anoint it and try to hide its skulls and crossbones. There must be a coming out; any kind of Christianity, however Orthodox it may sound, that does not major on the doctrine of coming out of the world is inadequate and imperfect.

After the word "out," we have the word "away." They came away from the old life, whatever that old life might have been. Coming away means different things to different people. But whatever it is, when we come to Jesus Christ to taste the good grace of God and that the Lord is gracious, there must be a coming away from the old life. Then naturally, there is a coming "unto" Christ. That, after all, is what the gospel is—a coming unto Christ.

Then there is the coming "together"; that is, they are coming unto each other. As we gather unto Christ, we gather unto each other, and the nearer we get to Christ, the nearer we get to each other. The way to get Christians together is not to form some kind of political united front but to bring them close to Jesus. If there were something down at the front of the church, some curio or missionary exhibit that I wanted to get you closer to, I would invite you to come down and see it. As you came unto it, you would come unto each other. The closer you got to it, the closer you would be to each other until, finally, shoulder would touch shoulder and you would be pushing close together to see this exhibit.

When we come unto Christ, we automatically come unto each other. That is why I have never been able to understand this monkish eremite attitude—the idea of going off by yourself to be a Christian to the exclusion of everyone else. There are people like that. They are antisocial or rather unsocial in disposition, so they do not like the fellowship of the saints.

If you are where Jesus is, you are surrounded by Jesus people; therefore, we ought to make the fellowship of the church the biggest thing in our lives. I would like to say right here, at the risk of hurting someone, that the important thing in the world today is the presence of an invisible spiritual entity called the Church, and the Holy Ghost never works outside that entity. He works through that entity in some manner or other. That is why I am a churchman.

A Sacred Nation

So we have those four phrases, "they came out of the world," "they came away from the old life," "they came unto Christ" and "they came together relative to each other." Peter said we come to Christ "as unto a living stone." This is a frequent Bible figure, this stone or rock, as it is sometimes called, and it almost invariably refers to a building. I think there may be a few places where David said "a great craggy rock where he hides." But for the most part, the figure has to do with the building; and because the Jews were a God-conscious people, their thoughts ran to a temple building. The Jewish nation, above all nations of the world, was a God-conscious nation.

America is not a God-conscious nation; we are a secular people. We have what the Bible calls a profane mind. And even in those who may toss God a bone when making a political speech to get the votes of a religious-minded people, if you probe in far enough you will find that our leadership is composed of a secular-minded people. I do not use the word in a wrong sense but in the sense that Esau was secular-minded. This world was the point of interest for that man, and that is all right for us, too, provided we have another and higher interest. But Esau did not have it, and the nation of America does not have it much; but Israel had it. Israel in fact had nothing else. Israel had no civil laws at all.

There was a time in England when she had two sets of laws: ecclesiastical laws and civil laws. For many centuries, a man could be tried before the civil law and then be turned loose and tried before the ecclesiastical law. The church could try a man for certain offenses and the civil law for certain other offenses.

There were two kinds of officers: civil officers and ecclesiastical officers. And there were two worlds mingling there, wheels within wheels. But not so in Israel. Israel had no civil officers; Israel had no civil law, no code of jurisprudence, no statutes on her books except those that were of God. The Bible was her code of law and her priests and scribes were her officials, and her high priests her leader, and her king anointed of God was her ruler. So Israel was a sacred nation, a people who were God-conscious more than any people that have ever lived in the world. Never has there been a nation as God-conscious as Israel.

We turn the telescope into the heavens, look at the stars and separate the stars from the God who made them. We call it astronomy. We dig into the rocks and have geology, and we monkey with little flying microscopic or submicroscopic matter and we have physics. We separate nature from God; but Israel never knew how to do that. God was everything. If an Israelite looked at a hill, it was God's hill; if he looked at a tree, the tree clapped its hands; and if he looked at the rain, it was God that sent the rain; and so a Jew never complained. If someone said, "It's miserable weather, isn't it?" God sent that rain, and God was in everything. When a figure of speech occurred, it was a divine figure of speech; and when they talked about a rock and stone, they were talking about a building that was a temple building.

The Living Stone

Israel had a temple building, of course, but it was composed of dead stones laid one upon another. They were hewn out and then laid one upon another and joined to each other by cutting and mortaring. That was a dead temple, and God knew it was a dead temple, and the only living thing in it was the Shekinah hanging between the wings of the golden cherubim. The temple itself was a dead thing. And our Lord knew it, pointed to its stones and said, "See ye not all these things? Verily I say unto you, There shall not be left here one stone upon another, that shall not be thrown down" (Matt. 24:2).

Through the years, they passed over it and even plowed the place where the temple had been. That is because it was a dead temple; but this new temple upon which we are come is composed of living stones; it is a living temple, and its cornerstone is Christ. Its stones are redeemed men and women who are alive by the gift of eternal life. He said, "Ye also are living stones."

I might point out that the *King James Version*, which is supposed to be always inerrant, makes a little mistake in 1 Peter 2:4-5. It says, "To whom coming, as unto a living stone . . . ye also, as lively stones." I wonder why the translators did that; in the Greek, it is exactly the same word. Both words mean "living." I imagine that when the translators were translating more than 400 years ago, the word "living" and "lively" meant the same thing. But today they do not.

"Lively" means what your boy is—popping around, never in one place twice. It means moving about so rapidly you cannot get it in one place long enough to count it. But that word "lively" has lost its meaning. It does not mean what it meant back there. It says the same thing about the church member as it says about the head of the Church, Jesus Christ. He is the living stone and the members that make up the great Temple are also living stones. There is a plural and a singular, but there is no difference in the adjective itself.

Israel had a dead temple made of dead stones. She could not use a Living Stone when she found one, and for that reason He was disallowed indeed of men, and Israel could not use Jesus Christ when He came. He was the living headstone of a new kind of temple, not one more stone to go in the old temple, but the headstone of a new kind of temple.

They looked at that stone and the builders shook their heads and said, "He doesn't fit anywhere; we have got our temple. There it stands, stone upon stone, tier upon tier, stone upon stone, stone joins a stone and its got a top on it and its there and it is set with beautiful jewels. Where does this man fit in?" Jesus Christ could not fit in, so Israel rejected Him and crucified Him because He was not shaped right. He was the stone that was to be the guided stone for the new temple to come, and He did not fit into the old temple at all. But God said that He was chosen and precious. Look at this stone.

I think it begins way back when Jacob had that sleep in the wilderness. He took up the stones of that place and set them for his pillow. When he saw that vision, he awoke out of his sleep, turned that stone over, stood it on end and anointed it, and it was called Bethel, the House of God. Then when Israel came out of Egypt, went into their wilderness and were traveling about those 40 years, that same stone followed them. If it was not the same chunk of rock, it was at least the same symbol, the same figure following through. So one day they were thirsty, and Moses smote the rock, and they all drank out of that same rock, at least symbolically, upon which Jacob had laid his head and anointed it and called it Bethel.

Then when our Lord came, He said that if you call upon this rock, you shall be saved, but if it falls upon you, you will be crushed. That was the same stone, and He said, "On this rock I will build my church." Let men say that rock is Peter, if they want to, but every figure, every type, every symbolism, every suggestion and every simile of the whole Bible indicates that that rock was none other than Jesus Christ Himself. In Daniel, we read of the rock of the stone cut out of the mountain without hands. That is the second coming of Jesus, when He comes back to rule in the earth. So there is our Savior, the Rock.

The Stones Built on the Living Rock

Now what is the function of the house built around this new rock? It contrasts with the Old Testament temple. The Old Testament temple was made of stones that were dead; but the New Testament temple is made of spiritual stones that are alive. The priest of the old temple walked into the temple and performed the functions of his office; but the priests of the New Testament *are* the temple.

There is the difference. We have a movable, portable temple, a temple made of living human beings, and every one of those human beings is a priest in his own right. That is why we do not need Father somebody. We have a High Priest, and that is why we do not go off to some telephone booth and sit and tell some old unmarried fellow about our troubles. Although we are priests in our own right, we have a great High Priest at the right hand of God. The temple of which we are a part is a temple of priests, so that we do not need to have anybody run interference for us when we go into the presence of God. We can come straight to Jesus Christ ourselves.

Some say that Jesus is too great and wonderful, and we cannot go to Him, but we can go to His mother, and she can help us. They say we do not have any pull with Jesus, but she has, and if we get to her and get her ear, she will go and have a talk with Jesus, and it will be all right.

We do not need her. She has performed her function, this lovely little Jewish lady. She brought into the world the man Christ Jesus and gave Him a body, which was later offered as a sacrifice on Calvary. She did her function when she brought Him up and fed Him at her breast and looked after Him and loved Him until He was a man. Then she passed out of the picture and Jesus Christ filled the horizon of believing men. But in our day, some are doing everything to make Jesus little and Mary big. I am dedicated to the magnification of Jesus Christ and making everybody else small by comparison.

We are priests, and we need no other priest to help us. This temple is a shrine where God dwells, and we offer not goats, not lambs, not doves, but spiritual sacrifices, says Peter—loving service and praise and song and worship.

Praise Offerings to Our Lord

The critics call us psalm singers. They called the old Scots people a bunch of psalm-singing Scotsmen. Those psalm-singing Scotsmen made their mark in the world. And our forebears, who once walked the rugged shores of New England and stamped America with their noble character, were psalm singers too. They met in little groups, in log buildings dedicated to worship, and there they sang psalms and offered the fruit of their lips—praises unto God. But they did not stop there. They shouldered their ax, went out and established cities and built a civilization the likes of which the world had never known. Those were the psalm-singing Puritans.

God hears psalms when they are sung in His name and for His glory. We offer up psalms to our Lord and songs and spiritual melodies in the Holy Ghost, and the critical and cynical world sees us close our eyes and talk to Someone we cannot see and says, "What is it all about?" We answer, "This is the temple of God, dedicated to the God of the temple, and we, the priests of the temple, sing these psalms to God the unseen and make our prayers to God the unseen." Though unseen He is real, and though unseen, He is nigh. We are not such fools as the world makes us out to be.

These praises, songs and spiritual sacrifices are acceptable to God. He accepted the Cornerstone; He accepted the living stones, which are gathered to the Cornerstone to make a temple for the Holy Ghost. If you have really prayed, if you have really sung a true song, if you have made your gifts out of the love of God, you have nothing visible to show for it. The world laughs and says, "You've nothing to show for all this."

Remember, not every precious thing shows at the same time it is received. There is a time when the invisible things will be the only real things and the visible world shall dissolve in smoke and pass away, and God will roll them up as a garment and as vestures they shall be changed. But the invisible things of God from the creation, which we have in Christ Jesus, will continue as real as heaven itself, forever and forever.

Are These Truths Alive in You?

The most important thing to determine is if this is true for you, *if so be that ye have tasted,* if so be that you have experienced that the Lord is gracious. The most vital thing to settle is not the truths of the Scriptures, for these have been established beyond question. The Scriptures are established by two immutable things: the resurrection of Jesus Christ from the dead and the coming down of the Holy Ghost. Everything hinges on Jesus Christ. The truth of the whole Word of God rests on the shoulders of Mary's Holy Son; and if He failed, the whole thing collapses around our ears. If He is who He said He is and He has risen from the dead, then He supports all the rest of the Bible itself.

That is why I am not afraid of modernists, of critics and higher critics, faultfinders and cynics. That is why I am not worried about Jonah and the Whale. I never spent five minutes in my life trying to decide whether a whale could swallow Jonah or not. God Almighty could make a whale that could swallow not only Jonah, but the whole ship and Nineveh thrown in. The point is not whether a whale swallowed Jonah; the point is what Jesus Christ said about it. He said, "For as Jonas was three days and three nights in the whale's belly, so shall the Son of man be three days and three nights in the heart of the earth" (Matt. 12:40). Jesus tied Himself up with the truth of the Jonah story. Therefore, the Jonah story is true because the Truth said it was.

Sometimes we are too apologetic with our apologetics. It does not rest upon us to determine whether the Bible is true or not. The resurrection of Jesus Christ and His ascension to the right hand of God and the coming of the Holy Ghost forever takes apologetics out of the hands of men and puts it in the hands of the Holy Spirit. We know the Bible is true not by long painful reasoning, but by a flash of inspiration from the throne and from the Holy Ghost that brings the flash.

The big problem is not whether the Bible is true. The big problem is whether it is true in you. It is not whether the Bible is true, but it is whether these things are true in you and me. Angelus Silesius (1624-1677), poet and priest, said:

Had Christ a thousand times,
Been born in Bethlehem,
But not in thee, thy sin
Would still thy soul condemn. . . .
Golgotha's cross from sin
Can never ransom thee,
Unless in thine own soul
It should erected be.

What we need to do today is go home, go to our room, open our Bible, get down on our knees and say, "Oh, God, are these things true of me?"

You can be a wonderfully nice person and still not be a true Christian. You can be a nice person and not be born again. You can be a nice religious person and never have tasted that the Lord is gracious. Let us search our own hearts. Let us see for ourselves if these things be so in us. A resurrected Savior and a down-coming Holy Ghost confirmed forever the fact that the Bible is true; but is it true in us? That is the big question. Search yourself and ask in the light of God's revealed truth, "Oh, God, I believe this; but is it true in me?" If it is not, it can be. Faith and repentance can make it real in your heart.

8

THE CHRISTIAN BELIEVES HE IS EXACTLY WHAT GOD SAYS HE IS

And a stone of stumbling, and a rock of offence, even to them which stumble at the word, being disobedient: whereunto also they were appointed. But ye are a chosen generation, a royal priesthood, an holy nation, a peculiar people; that ye should show forth the praises of him who hath called you out of darkness into his marvelous light: Which in time past were not a people, but are now the people of God: which had not obtained mercy, but now have obtained mercy.

1 PETER 2:8-10

I have always worked under the assumption that a bee can gather honey not only from a flower but also from a weed. For me, truth is truth no matter who says it or where it is found. I never disregard truth because it comes from an unexpected source.

If, for example, an atheist were to say that two plus two equals four, I would not disregard the truth because of the source. It does not matter who gives that equation; two plus two always equals four. I do not have to cuddle the source while embracing the truth.

One of the ancient philosophers of the past was quite compatible with the Christians of the first centuries, owing to the fact that truth is all one piece, and if a thing is true, it is true anyway. The early Christian church, by a kind of affinity, accepted one of those moral teachers not on the level of the inspired truth but as sort of a helpful side message. I refer to Epicurus (341–270 BC).

I give you one of his doctrines as an illustration of what I am to say to follow, and I give you only a running translation of it, rather than a verbatim translation. He said that the first thing about a man was that he was a human being. You could discover what a man ought to be by discovering the nature of the man, just as you can pick up a hammer, and if you are reasonably intelligent, deduce the purpose of the hammer by holding it in your hand. You would know that hammer was not shaped to saw a board or open a can of salmon. You could deduce from its shape that it was to be used to pound something. Or you could pick up a saw and deduce from the shape of the saw that the nature of the saw was not made to pound nails but to saw lumber.

Summing up the old philosopher, we deduce from the nature of man what kind of person or what kind of being he ought to be. To be a man is the first responsibility of a human being. Epicurus settled that we can know our duties, and that is as far as Epicurus went. The Bible has little to say about duties and privileges. But he said we could know our duties by figuring out what we are and the facets of our humanity, our manhood, and which way they turned.

For instance, settling that you are a human being, your highest privilege and responsibility is to develop yourself as a human being. Following that, you can know what that development is by considering your relationships. First, you are a son or a daughter, which implies certain obligations and duties and responsibilities toward your parents. If you are a husband or wife, the fact of wifehood or husbandhood implies certain responsibilities toward your mate. And the fact that you are a citizen implies certain responsibilities toward the state. That you are a father implies certain responsibilities among your children, and so on.

With that as a little backdrop of illustration, let me point out what Peter said: "You are a chosen generation, a royal priesthood, a holy nation, a peculiar people." Epicurus said that the first thing is that you are a man; then after that you figure out your responsibilities as a man. Peter said the first thing about you is that you are a Christian. He takes the manhood for granted and begins where Epicurus ended. He says that we are born again (or begotten again) "unto a [living] hope by the resurrection of Jesus Christ from the dead" (1 Pet. 1:3). He does not begin with our basic humanity; he begins with our basic Christianity. Then he goes on to show that, as Christians, there are at least four facets to our nature and four relationships.

There are four things that you are, just as Epicurus's man is a husband or a citizen or both; just as he has his various relationships, so, as a Christian, you have various relationships.

You are, as a Christian, a number of things, and you can figure out your duty and your privileges by seeing what you are.

A Chosen Generation

As a Christian, you belong to a company that God calls a "chosen generation." He applied all the terms of the Old Testament Israel to the New Testament Church, only He raised them up to another level and made them spiritual. Israel was called the chosen seed. In the hymn "All Hail the Power of Jesus' Name" (Edward Perronet, 1726-1792), we sing, "Ye chosen seed of Israel's race, ye ransomed from the fall." And Peter says, "You Christians have various facets to your nature." There are various things you are, and one of them is that you are a chosen generation.

That word "generation" does not mean a descent in the sense that we mean it, nor does it mean a time such as when we say "this generation." But it means a breed—if you will allow that rather ugly word for such a wonderful thing as being born of God; it means a breed, a species. He says that you Christians are a chosen species; you are a new breed of human. We start with your humanity but we go on to your new birth, and that constitutes a new breed of humans as completely different from the fallen race of Adam as though you belong on another world. "You are a chosen breed, a chosen generation of people." That is what we are; and just as Epicurus's man would figure out his responsibilities to the state by remembering that he is a citizen, so we Christians can figure out our responsibilities and privileges by remembering that we are a new breed of human.

I know the world will laugh at that and they have good reason to laugh at the way some of us act. We act very much like the old barnyard scrubs we used to be. But God said we are, nevertheless, a "new, a chosen, generation." We are a select generation. Just as men select breeds and produce the finest, God has produced a select generation, not by building on Adam, but by rebirth from above. He has created a new generation of humans. And He said with it come responsibilities and privilege. You can figure out how to be and the kind of person you ought to be by remembering who you are.

If only God's people could remember who they are. We let the world tell us what we are. We let our government tell us what we are. To the world, we are simply religious people; to our government, we are taxpayers and voters. But God says we are more than that. We are citizens, and as citizens, we have always paid taxes. We pay taxes whether we vote or not; but we are more than that. We are a chosen generation; the real born-again Christian faith belongs to a new school of thought, a new level of humanity, a new breed of humanity. Having been born from above, we are still being human. Christians are a twice-born human generation.

A Royal Priesthood

That ought to give us pause and food for thought . . . what kind of people we are to be. But Peter says more. He said you are also "a royal priesthood." That was familiar to the Old Testament people; they had a priesthood and understood the ramifications. Those who could approach God officially, who could approach God for the people, were the priests, and they came out of only one line—the tribe of Levi. Not all could be priests, for even Jesus could not have been an Old Testament priest for the simple reason that He belonged to the line of Judah, and not of Levi. But they knew what a priesthood was. It consisted of a certain order of men who offered sacrifices, made prayers and stood between God and the people as a priesthood. Now he says, "You are a priesthood." You Christians are now a priesthood.

That is the other facet of your nature. You are a priest, and not only a priest, but also a royal priest. The priests of the Old Testament were not royal priests. The royal line was Judah, and the priestly line was the Levitical line. The two lines never crossed. The New Testament Christian is neither Judah nor Levi (nor Dan, nor any of the other lines). He is of a new order of humans, twice-born human, and one of his functions is to act as a priest. Because he is born of royal seed, Jesus, he is a royal priest.

Think of yourself like that, and do not let the world or the books of psychology tell you what you are. Go to God's Word and find out what you are as a believing man or woman and as a Christian, a follower of Christ. You belong to a royal priesthood, and the priesthood now lies in the hands of the individual Christians. It is not an order of part of the people; the church is the priesthood, and every Christian is his own priest. That is very hard for some people to understand.

Because every Christian is a royal priest before God, we do not need the priest of the Old Testament temple. We do not need the priest of Buddha or of the Catholic Church. We need no priest because we are ourselves priests. Priests do not go to priests for help. We are our own priests and are constituted so by virtue of the fact that we belong to a new order of humans. We are a new breed of the human race. We are still part of the old humans, but we are new humans through Christ, and the day will come when the old humanity will pass away as the co-coon passes away from the butterfly, and all that you are and that you spend so much money and time on and boast about will all pass away. You will shed that old Adamic generation as a cocoon and will spring up into a new life. Only the new will be alive forevermore, and the old shall die and pass away. So we are a new generation and a chosen one; but we are also a royal priesthood.

A Holy Nation

Then Scripture says you are a "holy nation." The church here is thought of as a nation. If Jesus Christ is our Lord and King, and if Israel is a holy nation in the midst of the nations, but not part of the nation, so the church, the true church of Christ, is a holy nation dwelling in the midst of the nations, but not part of the nations.

I recommend that you sit down sometime and think about what you are. Just think about it. You say you do not want to get interested in yourself. Well, you had better, because the devil is, and the world is, and so you had better be interested too. If you are a believer in Christ, you'd better sit down, and in the presence of God, quietly think with the Scriptures open before you about what you are as a born-again man and what the different relationships are that you hold and what facets of your nature there are.

One facet is that you belong to a separated nation. "Holy" has to do with ceremonially separated as well as morally pure. And just as Israel dwelt in the middle of the nations as part of the world but not part of the nations, so we now as a new priesthood, a royal priesthood, compose a nation, a new nation, a spiritual nation within the world without being affected by the world.

Take a globe of the world and turn it so that the most land area is visible and the least water area, so that right in the geographic center of that vast land area would be Palestine. God said His nation was in the midst of the earth, and He meant what He said, and Israel was a nation apart. But off to the south and to the north and east and the west were other nations; but by carefully defined boundaries Israel lived as a people apart in the midst of the nations. Her curse came when she forgot her holy national status and began to intermarry and intermingle with the world round about her, and God turned that same world loose on her, and their armies came in and destroyed her so that Jerusalem was destroyed 70 times in history.

If you think of what you are as a Christian, you belong to a holy nation. You cannot afford to fuss with any of the nationals in this new race and new priesthood, this new nation. You cannot afford to have anything at odds with anybody, but love everybody and live in harmony so far as you are able to, because you are part of a nation, and a holy nation separated from the world.

Christianity in our day does not see this as clearly as they could. We try to dovetail in and gear in and blend in, and the sharp outlines are gone, and nothing but a cowardly blending remains. God stood the light on one side and said, "Let there be light." On the other side He said, "Let there be darkness." And He called the one, day, and the other, night, and God has meant that division to be down the years. But we are living in an unholy twilight where there can be discovered very little of that holy light and not too much that is holy. Darkness or even sin has taken some of the shining robes of Christianity and disguised it as filthiness. But God's people ought to see to it that they are what God says they are—a holy nation, a separated nation living in the midst of the world but absolutely apart from it.

A Peculiar People

Then the fourth facet he said was that we are a "peculiar people." "Peculiar," as used 350 years ago, meant a people for a position, a bought people, a purchased people. It has a different meaning now. "Peculiar" now means someone doing strange things; someone with idiosyncrasies, a personality problem and erratic personality problems. But that is not what the Bible means by "peculiar." The meaning in the Bible is a purchased people. This was true of Israel back in the Deuteronomy setting. They were purchased by the blood of the sacrificial lamb and brought out as a peculiar people taken unto God Himself. That is what Christians are.

The world accuses Christians of being bigoted people, full of pride, who think they can claim to be the people of God. The world says, "Is not God the Father of all men?" The answer is no. Do not try to apologize; just say no. Do not quote four or five authorities and soften it down. Just say no, because you know that God is not the Father of all people. He is the Father of such as believe in the Lord Jesus Christ. He takes this new breed of people, this people born from above, and constituted as a royal priesthood and a chosen generation and a peculiar people, unto Himself in the way that the peoples of the world are never taken.

You have a perfect right to stand on God's truth about that. And if they say, "Who do you think you are?" Just say, "I know who I am, by the mercy of God, because He says that 'which in time past were not a people, but now are the people of God: which had not obtained mercy, but now have obtained mercy'" (1 Pet. 2:10). You can write this verse in the back of your wallet or engrave it on the tablets of your heart, because this is you, if you are a true Christian.

As Christians, we ought to think of ourselves as being what God says we are. We cannot allow false modesty, doubts or unbelief to prevent us from accepting God's favor and putting ourselves in faith and humility where God puts us. If we are not there, we can get there, for the door of mercy stands wide open for all who come.

Christians are a people for God's own possession. They are a peculiar people, a marked-off people, constituting a nation apart of priests, royal priests, rising out of this new thing that is born in the midst of the earth, the Church. We are exactly what God says we are. No more, and certainly no less.

9

THE CHRISTIAN'S LIFE AMONG NON-CHRISTIANS

Dearly beloved, I beseech you as strangers and pilgrims, abstain from fleshly lusts, which war against the soul.

1 PETER 2:11

The church of Jesus Christ is flooded with people assuming authority from God that they do not really have. Whether this is a misunderstanding of Scripture or a simple defect in personality is beyond my comprehension. But I do know that not all boasts are rooted in Scripture.

Peter, as an apostle, had every authority that God ever gave to any man on earth . . . greater authority even than that enjoyed by Moses, because it was broader. And yet, Peter did not command these Christians scattered abroad but beseeched them and called them by a tender term of affection. "Dearly beloved, I beseech you."

The reason is that there are certain moral acts that cannot be secured by commandments. Certain other ones can. It is altogether possible to command, "Thou shalt not kill," because the act of murder can be restrained, and if we do not kill another, then we have fulfilled the commandment, and a human life has been saved. But there are certain other acts, which must be voluntarily obeyed if they are to be real, because willingness is a part of their moral content so that threats and force cannot work to secure these ends.

Be Willing to Remain Separate

If Peter had said, "I command you that you walk as pilgrims and strangers and avoid fleshly lust," he would have been commanding an impossibility. To know the character of a pilgrim and a stranger and to live before God in weak humility and purity, which overrides the desires of the flesh, is something that can only be achieved by a spiritual willingness; therefore, it cannot be commanded.

Allow me to illustrate it like this. A man can come home from his work a brutal, coarse man and walk up to his wife and with an angry face threaten her and say, "What's the reason dinner is not on the table?" and command her to get his dinner. She is afraid of him and knows he does have some kind of legal hold on her, so she hurries off and puts the dinner on the table. He gets his dinner by commandment, but he cannot walk up to that same woman and say, "I command you to love me." He cannot get love by commandment, because willingness and inward participation of a voluntary kind are necessary to love but are not necessary to the obedience to a commandment. The man of God did not say, "I command"; he said, "I beseech you therefore, brethren, by the mercies of God, that ye give your bodies as a living sacrifice, holy, acceptable unto God" (Rom. 12:1). The nature of this consecration was such that they had to do it willingly and without reprisal or sanction or they could not have done it at all.

Peter explained to them that Christians are strangers on earth. The word "stranger," as Peter uses it here, is "sojourner." Usually, it refers to someone temporarily living in a foreign country, not at home there and not intending to be, and separated from the natives by language and dress and customs and conduct and usually by culture. The stranger is a person from a foreign country who is not at home where he is and is not going to settle down and be at home there but is temporarily in that country. He is separated by language, so he speaks with an accent. He is separated by dress, custom, conduct, diet and culture. This makes him a stranger.

America does not know too many strangers; we absorb them too fast. We melt them up so fast that we hardly know they are. As soon as they get over their first original thi... are American. But the Bible here recognizes sojo... where they were only there for a time. It is so... men with the United Nations in New York... there temporarily and have no intention of... taking out naturalization papers; they are s... there for a time, separated by language and... duct, and past and tradition and memories...

Don't Get Comfortab...

Just as soon as a man ceases to be separated... him, he is a stranger no more. But Peter n...

becoming naturalized or getting over our character as strangers. As Christians, we are strangers on earth.

Abraham and Lot are outstanding examples of how men can be strangers and then cease to be strangers. Abraham and Lot came from Ur of the Chaldees and entered into the land of Palestine. One day their herdsmen quarreled, and Abraham and Lot got together, like two relatives should, talked it over and decided they had better separate. They were too big to grow together anymore, and there was bad blood between their servants. So Abraham said, "You look it over and go the way you want to go and I'll take what's left." So, selfish man that he was, Lot looked toward the plains of Jordan and moved down that direction. Abraham stayed on the plains of Mamre, where there was some grass but not too much.

The man Lot went where the grass was green and pitched his tent toward Sodom. It was not long until he sat in the gate which is equivalent to saying that if he was not the ity, at least he was high up in an official position, d their offices in the gate of the city as we have e day some other kings came along, made an ity and captured the city and Lot and his

eone who escaped came looking for help. ? Lot was in no position to help; he was one ple. Where did they look for the help they rticular situation? They said, "We'll go tell ew."

ew means "stranger." The only man capable risis was the man who never identified himself with them but rather separated from them. Only someone outside of them could rescue them from their dilemma. So they sent for Abraham, not Lot. Lot was already handcuffed and tied up and hamstrung like a hog taken to market. Lot, who sat in the gate, was now lying in the back end of a wagon somewhere, being carried away like so much hamburger. They had to send for Abraham, the stranger, who had kept himself free from Sodom and all of its people. Abraham got his little army, went out and defeated the enemy and rescued Lot and his people.

Another example. Two Christians start out together and one of them gets involved in the things of this world. He loses his character as a stranger. He may rise to a place where he sits in the gate, but he loses something that the other man has. The other man withdraws and keeps himself separated as far as possible from the ways of the world and lives the separated life of a stranger. Then trouble comes and someone down the street gets in a jam. Which one do they send for? Lot, the assimilator? No, he is in as much trouble as the rest. They always send for the man who has been separated and kept separated, Abraham.

Just Passing Through

Peter said, "Not only are you Christians strangers, but you are pilgrims as well." A pilgrim is a stranger on his way from one place to another. A pilgrim is someone passing through en route. Always remember that a Christian is en route. He is not where he started and he is not where he is going; he is only where he is now.

Sometimes a man will visit Chicago and call me and say, "This is so and so." Either I will know him or not. He will introduce himself or some friend I know, usually a preacher, writer or something, and I say, "Oh, you're visiting Chicago?"

"No, just on the way through from Detroit or Cleveland [or somewhere else] and on my way to Omaha or Denver on west."

He is just en route. He has his ticket in his pocket and just stopped to speak to a friend on his way through. That is the character of a pilgrim. That is what it means—somebody en route, somebody passing through. Somebody not settling down. This is the Christian concept of things. Heaven is our fatherland toward which we are journeying, and earth is a wilderness.

Christians are often chided for their concept of the world as being a "veil of tears." I have read some very caustic criticisms of that Christian concept. "What kind of gloomy old crows are you sitting around croaking about this veil of tears?" But that is the Christian concept, take it or leave it. The world in which we live is, because of sin, a temporary visitation that sin has made; it is a wilderness through which we journey, and we may rest awhile but only for a night. Then we pitch our tent a day's march nearer home. But we are never to settle here, and we are never to become naturalized.

I often spend time just going through the hymnbook noticing this idea that Christians are strangers on their way to heaven. Let me quote just a few brief excerpts from some great hymns. John Mason Neale (1818-1866) wrote:

O happy band of pilgrims,
if onward ye will tread
with Jesus as your fellow
to Jesus as your Head!

The reverend John Samuel Bewley Monsell (1811-1875) wrote one stanza in the hymn "On Our Way Rejoicing" that I particularly enjoy:

On our way rejoicing gladly let us go;
Conquered hath our Leader, vanquished is our foe;
Christ without, our safety, Christ within, our joy;
Who, if we be faithful, can our hope destroy?

And everybody remembers this famous Welch song "Guide Me, O Thou Great Jehovah," by William Williams (1717-1791):

Guide me, O Thou great Jehovah,
Pilgrim through this barren land;
I am weak, but Thou art mighty,
Hold me with Thy pow'rful hand.
Bread of heaven, Bread of heaven,
Feed me till I want no more;
Feed me till I want no more.

John Cennick (1718-1755) wrote the following in "Children of the Heavenly King":

We are traveling home to God,
In the way our fathers trod;
They are happy now, and we
Soon their happiness shall see.

And in 1721, Nikolaus L. von Zinzendorf (1700-1760) wrote:

Jesus, still lead on,
Till our rest be won!

And although the way be cheerless,
We will follow, calm and fearless.
Guide us by thy hand
To our Fatherland.

That is just a sampling. You can find similar words by the dozens written by those who conceive their earth to be a wilderness through which the Christian pilgrim travels on his way to the fatherland. But he is not alone; the person of the Lord Jesus Christ is always the unseen One walking by his side and within him. The pilgrim may have to stop and pitch his tent overnight; he may have to assume the character of a soldier and fight his way through; but always he is en route.

Let Your Inner Life Lead You

While you are en route, "abstain from fleshly lusts, which war against the soul" (1 Pet. 2:11). These fleshly lusts are those natural appetites that have their seed in the body and the mind. These natural appetites would be innocent except for sin, but are now enemies of the soul.

Here is one of those instances where you cannot command anybody; you can only beseech them as pilgrims and strangers. But we may be sure of this: Anyone who is going to make his journey safely and successfully will have to keep himself free from those fleshly lusts that war against the soul. If we do not, we will be slowed down or stopped in our tracks. The inner life must overcome the flesh or the flesh will overcome and destroy the inner life. It is strange and deplorable but true that one part of us fights against another part of us. That is the law of nature;

it fights against the higher nature. The flesh fights against the spirit and the fleshly lusts war against our soul. Thomas à Kempis said, "Peace will always be found not in indulging our lower appetites but in resisting them."

Ralph Waldo Emerson (1803-1882), a mere philosopher, not a Christian at all (but a great thinker) said this: "Every victory we win over the flesh, however slight, will prove to be a strengthening act to our souls." We are pilgrims journeying home, and the only real enemies, the only dangerous enemies, are within us. God has changed the lions on the outside. God has said to Satan, "This far and no farther." God has spoken to the very armies of the world and forbade them to touch His anointed; to bring to His prophet any harm. We have within us temptations, which if yielded to would destroy our soul. So says the Holy Ghost, "I beseech you as strangers and pilgrims, abstain from fleshly lusts, which war against the soul."

10

THE CHRISTIAN'S PRESENCE AMONG THE UNSAVED

Having your conversation honest among the Gentiles: that, whereas they speak against you as evildoers, they may by your good works, which they shall behold, glorify God in the day of visitation.

1 PETER 2:12

Any earnest Christian must settle one important question in his life: What should be my attitude toward the Gentiles? By Gentiles, we simply mean the unsaved among whom we live. What should be my attitude toward the unsaved with whom I am forced most of my lifetime to live? When I say most of my lifetime, I am not speaking lightly, but accurately, because, though Christians tend to flock together, still a greater part of a Christian's time on earth is likely spent among the Gentiles.

One of the primary characteristics of Christians is the tendency to flock together. They come together in various meetings here and there; anything from the lowly Sunday School picnic to the High Mass. Christians have a marvelous habit of flocking together. Real Christians flock together, and the reasons are many and very full, I believe.

Our Natural Affinity for Salt

In the first place, Christians belong to another racial group. "Ye are a chosen generation, a different breed, you are a royal priesthood, a holy nation, a peculiar people." Thus, we form another sort of racial group within the race into which we were born. We are strangers but not strangers to each other, and therefore it is perfectly natural that human beings should want to go with their own group, because they understand each other's language.

I can understand why Polish, Swedish, Lithuanian and even German people tend to be clannish. We say, "They're clannish," and smile. But it is not clannish so much as they like to hear somebody talk that does not talk with an accent. They want to get among people who can bless their ears with that first sound they heard when they were born across the water or when they were old enough to hear sounds and knew what they meant, and so those sounds blessed their ears with good speech.

Groups tend to get together because they love the sound of it, and Christians love to get together because they understand each other's language.

Not only are we another racial group, but we are also another family, and families always like to get together. Families like to get together; and out in the country regions where they are less sophisticated, family reunions are a great time when all those who are remotely related to that crowd will come together and sit around and talk; and some have never met the other ones; new ones have been born in the previous year. These families like to get together. They have a lot in common. There is a tie that belongs to the family that belongs nowhere else on earth.

So we Christians belong to the same family; we are the household of God. And God is our Father after whom every family in heaven and earth is named. So that is why Christians love to get together.

People who share similar interests enjoy getting together. When they are among people of like interests there is much to talk about. It does not matter if it is a hobby or sports or politics or philosophy, people like to talk about things that interest them. Therefore, they like to be around people who share the same interests.

Just imagine a person who literally hates sports finding himself among a group of people who only talk about sports. There is no common interest and, therefore, there is no fellowship. But let that same person find himself in a crowd of people who love the same things he does, and watch the fellowship flow. This is what is behind Christian fellowship. This is why Christians love to get together; and when they get together, there is a great deal of mutual interest and camaraderie.

People also get together because of the moral encouragement that comes to a minority group by having the presence of other members of that minority group around them.

Out of the Saltshaker

So, for all those reasons, we love to get together. However, it still remains true that the average Christian spends a greater part of his life on earth among the Gentiles. He spends the greater number of hours and days and months and years among people that are not sympathetic with them, that do not believe as he believes and are not saved.

Take the workplace for instance. Some never see a Christian from the time they leave their house in the morning until they return at night. If they do, they do not know they are Christians. You see someone walking down the street who may be a Christian, but you do not know it; it means nothing to you at the moment, so you literally live among the Gentiles from the time you say good-bye in the morning until you come home at night. And worse than that, some never see a Christian from the time they say goodbye to friends at the church door Sunday evening until Wednesday or the next Sunday, because even in their home there are no Christians.

I was searching my memory to remember how many Christians I have met traveling on the trains. I have traveled quite a little bit over the United States, and I think I only remember one Christian that I thought, "There is a man of God." He was a porter. He talked to me when he saw me reading my Bible. I always have my Bible, my notebooks and pens and a desk, and they all know it. But I have never had a porter but once ever comment smilingly with appreciation about me having my Bible. You do not find them when you travel as a rule.

How many Christians did you purchase something from this week? And if you are selling, how many Christians did you sell to? Now, if you happen to work for some Christian group, you probably did sell to some Christians; but for the most part, your buying and selling is not with Christians.

And in school, if you have a classroom maybe with 30 or 40 in it, how many are Christians in that group? How many of you have Christians living next door to you? How many Christians are in your block where you live? Think now, not very many of them. Occasionally you will find a couple of houses where both are Christians, but very rarely. Mostly, God salts us down as we shake salt in the earth. Salt is every place but we do not touch each other for we are scattered for most of the time; and, therefore, because we spend a few hours a week with Christians and spend many, many hours a week with the unsaved, it is vitally important that we have the answer to the question, What should my attitude be toward the unsaved?

As usual, God lays it down here in a broad precept; He does not give the details. He says, "Have your conversation honest among the Gentiles." Other translations have it as "seemly, good and right; beyond reproach and upright; let your conduct be seemly. Let it be honest, let it be good and right, let it be beyond reproach, let it be upright." Various translators use all those words in an attempt to get the meaning of the Greek word that Peter used. The application is left to the circumstance, the time and the individual.

God's Recipe for a Piquant Life

God never tells us anything that will enable us to get along without Him. God lays down what we read in our Scripture lesson precepts. He lays down broad principles and then allows the moment, the situation, the circumstances, the individual and the context to determine how those principles shall be applied. Therefore, it is never right to take the attitude that many do, "Well, I have my Bible, I know what to do, here it is, it's found in verse 9. I know what to do, I have the answer."

That is the attitude of unspiritual Orthodoxy—always sure of the answer, it knows because it can quote the text. Remember, the text is only the broad precept. The application of it takes the living presence of the Holy Ghost. It takes humility, faith, earnest prayer and often painful cross-carrying in order to bring that precept into life and make it apply.

Orthodoxy says, "I know the answer, here it is in seven tenets." But the humble Christian knows better. He knows he has the tenets there and subscribes to them as ardently as any man, but how to apply them at a given time and context takes the Holy Ghost, prayer, humility, sometimes fasting, more prayer and sacrifice.

Being sound in the faith does not mean that God has tossed the Bible to you and says, "Here's the rule book, goodbye. Follow the rules and you'll make it through the gates at last." Never, never. God says, "Here is the rule book; here are the precepts for righteousness. Do not get puffed up now, because you are a weak person and situations change like the chance of circumstance, so you will never quite know how to orientate yourself. You lean on Me hard, you trust Me constantly, you pray all the time, because otherwise you will not know how to make that precept apply in the hour when you need it."

Always remember, God never tells you anything enabling you to get along without Him. And if you were to memorize the whole Bible by heart, you would still need the presence of God and the living influence of the Holy Ghost living within you to enable you to live even a tiniest verse of that Bible. So always

God suspends us in space. We always like to get everything nailed down, get a marker there and put up a plaque; and when friends come, be able to point and say, "There's my religion, look at that, isn't that solid, four legs solid on the floor, solid, there it is." We like it that way and we like to get hold of our verses and then say, "I know how to run my life." God says, "No, My child, you only know the broad outline. The details must be filled in by prayer and faith and humility."

The broad precept He lays down here for the attitude of the Christian. He says, "Be honest among the Gentiles, be seemly and good and right and beyond reproach and upright." Those are broad, there are no details given, but this is at the beating heart of it. This is first, because it is indispensable. You can know all the rules in the book, but unless you live a life that is honest and seemly and beyond reproach, it will mean nothing to the Gentiles.

Those with an Aversion to the Taste of Salt

The *Phillips* translation uses a phrase I like: "Although they may in the usual way slander you" (1 Pet. 2:12). There is something sadly humorous about that. "Although they may in the usual way slander you as evil-doers, yet when disasters come, they may glorify God when they see how well you conduct yourselves." Those Christians in Peter's day expected to be slandered. It was standard procedure.

Their Hostility

Why do the unsaved Gentiles want to slander Christians? I believe they do it for a number of reasons.

For example, the once-born react instinctively against the twice-born. Most people, even Christians, do not understand this, and not very many people are talking about it, but it is true. If God would send a worldwide revival, this would become obvious, that the once-born instinctively react in hostility toward the twice-born. It started back in the beginning with Cain and Abel. Cain reacted hostilely against Abel. Cain the once-born reacted in enmity toward the twice-born. It repeated itself with two other brothers, Isaac and Ishmael. Ishmael persecuted Isaac. The seed of the bondwoman persecuted the seed of the free woman by a natural hostility. This still prevails today.

Their Automatic Rejection

Scientists used to use a phrase they called "natural enmity." There are certain creatures that instinctively fear other creatures. Even though they have been raised in a zoo or brought up around a house and have never seen those creatures, they instinctively fear them. Every hunter knows that if he rides a horse and it begins trembling, rears, snorts and whinnies, he can be sure that it is one of the horse's natural enemies, usually the bear. The horse knows the presence of a bear, just the smell of the bear over the next hill. He does not have to see him; and even though he is a young colt and never been out hunting before and has never been within smelling distance of a bear, he goes all to pieces when he smells that bear. Every hunter knows that. That is natural enmity. There is something in that horse that fears and hates that bear; and it is not experience, but its natural reaction.

The world may never have seen a Christian. When missionaries first entered China back in the days of Robert Jaffrey and

William Glover, they were called foreign devils and lived at the peril of their lives continually. The first instinctive reaction of Confucianism China was to react in hostility against the Christian because he was born again. The Christian was not doing him any harm; he was just there. It is because the Christian has one spirit, the Gentiles have another, and those spirits will never get together. They can never compromise.

Christ had in Him one Spirit, and all the world around Him had another; and no matter what simple, innocent thing Christ did, they were on Him in a minute, not because of what He did, or of what He said, but because of what He was.

So count on it. When something like this is mentioned, some people worry that it will discourage young people from becoming a Christian. If you tell them that if they become Christian and the world will be against them, you will discourage them. Truth never stopped God's work, and to tell the truth, never prevented anybody from being a Christian. It is a terrible deception presenting only a half-Christianity to a young person; and then when the pressure comes and the spitballs begin to fly in his direction, he loses heart and quits, and we call him a backslider. No, he is not a backslider; he is someone that never knew what he had hold of or what had hold of him. Tell them the truth from the beginning.

Their Jealousy

Then there is the matter of jealousy. Christians put the unsaved people to shame, and consequently, they are jealous of them. Cain was jealous of Abel. In their hostile attitude, I notice a bit of bravado or bluster really, and simulated enmity; but underneath there is a secret longing to be like the Christian.

As a young man of 17, I was saved and I walked by the crowds on my way to church and did not mingle too much with that group of unsaved people. One of them was converted afterward and said to me, "You know the thing that moved my heart and put me under conviction? Just your going and coming amongst us; but you didn't mingle. You just went and came, and it put me under conviction." They could say funny things and make cracks, but underneath was a gnawing uncertainty.

The Unmistakable Savor of Christ in You

The presence of an honest Christian living an upright life in the midst of the Gentiles is God's most powerful instrument to condition men for the gospel of His Son, Jesus Christ. A lot of this hostility is merely bravado, and a lot of big talk is just bluster. Really, in their secret hearts, God put eternity there—even in the sinner's heart—and he is not satisfied when he thinks somebody else has gotten hold of that for which he was born, and he has not gotten it yet. He will be mad and will say unpleasant things and slander, but the Scripture says they see your good works.

Moral beings cannot successfully argue for long against righteousness. Adolph Hitler tried defying all moral laws, turning righteousness into sin and sin into righteousness. He roared louder over the airways than any other man has roared since the days of the bulls of Dashan, and his great armies went out. But where is Hitler today? Poor, staggering, tired, heartsick Germany is trying to find again the righteousness of her reformers, trying where she can to find again the things she threw recklessly away under the meddling of that roaring bull.

A nation cannot argue very long against righteousness. You cannot successfully argue the validity of evil to a moral people, even an unsaved people who have a certain morality within them. When they see your good works, you have taken away their weapons; you have taken their gun out of their hand and thrown it in the ditch. They will argue, they will bluster, they will strut, they will condemn and slander "as usual," but they are not convinced by their own loud talk. You have convinced them by your good life.

At last, Peter says, "And what will ye do in the day of visitation, and in the desolation which shall come from far? To whom will ye flee for help? And where will ye leave your glory?" (Isa. 10:3). Translators do not know which of two things is meant here, and neither do I. So, I will give you both. Whether he means by the day of visitation the time of trouble on earth or whether he means the Day of Judgment when the Lord visits men's sins upon themselves, I do not know. I do not claim to know. I do not think it can be discovered what Peter had in mind. I do not know, but he may have had both or either in mind. So the very person that is against you in the day of his trouble will be forced to glorify God for you. I do not know whether that can mean Day of Judgment or not. I would rather think it might mean in the day of trouble when poor Job was visited with his tribulation, and others have been visited with tribulation.

The Influence of a Steady, Quiet Faith

There is a strange truth about living among the Gentiles. If a well-known Christian brother is living down the block here, everybody round about smiles, shrugs and says, "He is a fanatic.

He goes to a good gospel church and spends his time in prayer. He is a good fellow, but there is surely something cracked there." All up and down the block, there are church people, but no Christians, just church people. One comes out of his place in the morning and starts to church. He looks like a Stanley Steamer because he is giving off fumes as he goes; and another fellow goes off to another church, but nobody is living right. One Christian in the block, everybody knows how he lives, he is kidded about it, but everybody knows how he lives. Now, let somebody suddenly get into a great crisis, let something happen to somebody in that block, who do they send for? They always send for the man of God, always.

Much can be said in favor of just living things down. Just stay around and do not get impatient; and if you will just live right long enough in your block, you will be slandered a little, but when trouble comes, you will be called in. It is always so. They say, "Oh, we love Father so and so, he plays cards with us, he drinks with us, he smokes with us, he can even tell you dirty jokes, occasionally he's a funny fellow, I don't know where he gets all those jokes." All right, let some critical thing happen in the home and if they know where there is somebody that can pray, they will send for him and not the man who can tell them a dirty joke.

People go to a doctor and say, "Doctor, I feel all run down; what do you recommend?" One doctor says, "Well, straighten up, live right, eat the proper diet, get enough sleep and in six months' time you won't know yourself." We shrug him off.

"Oh, doctor, that sounds old-fashioned. Don't you have something I can take? I want to feel better tomorrow." Therefore, he patiently gives us some pills we take and psychologically we think we are better, but we are not. Americans are impatient, and the same goes with American Christianity. Some people now want Christianity in the form of a pill, something that will work very quickly.

God says, "Don't get so anxious, you've got eternity to live in. Just live it out. Just work it out, sweat it out, stay around, live right, let week follow week and month follow month, and keep right and keep praying, and you'll win."

"But, God, I want to win today."

How about the eleventh chapter of Hebrews? Some of those old saints believed God and died without seeing anything happen much. But they all died in faith. So God wants you to live in faith; and if you need to, die in faith. You will win at last; and when you go, you will leave a sweet fragrance behind you. They can break or shatter the vase, but the scent of the roses will hang around still. You will wonder about your family. I wonder about mine; my brother, my sister, my relatives, in-laws. I wonder about them. I don't know much I can do, but I do know one thing. If I live right and walk before them as I should, I am putting up an argument they cannot successfully dispute; and perhaps if I just live it through, they will glorify God in the day of visitation.

11

THE CHRISTIAN'S RELATION TO GOVERNMENT AND AUTHORITY

Submit yourselves to every ordinance of man for the Lord's sake:
whether it be to the king, as supreme; or unto governors, as unto them
that are sent by him for the punishment of evildoers, and for the praise
of them that do well. For so is the will of God, that with well doing ye
may put to silence the ignorance of foolish men: as free, and not using
your liberty for a cloak of maliciousness, but as the servants of God.

1 PETER 2:13-16

Human government is a divine order. This is far beyond the old doctrine of the divine right of kings, which placed kings over their people as a god and gave them full authority of deciding life and death. They could be as arbitrary, as contrary, as cruel and as oppressive as they chose and be justified in it on the grounds that no one had a right to complain against the anointed of the Lord. That is one thing, but that is not what the Bible teaches about human government.

In Genesis 9, the Bible clearly lays down that the idea of the first ruler in human government, as from the Lord, and developed from the family idea—of the father as the paternal source of the family and thus head of the family, and naturally its protector, defender and breadwinner. This idea was of someone who has a right to do it, who earns that right by protecting, defending and winning a living for the family. Then it spread to the tribe as developed in the books of the Old Testament, and then to the village and then to the largest city, and in some instances, the city was the government itself, as was Athens and Sparta. It developed further to the nations, and finally to empires.

In the Bible, the king idea is very prominent. In fact, it is only fair to say that there is not any other kind of government recognized in the Bible except the government of a head, usually called a king, over an obedient and happy people. The word "king," curiously enough, comes from the word "kin."

In the North, you rarely hear the word "kinfolk" or "kin" used. But in the South, it is very common to say, "None of my kinfolk are living," or "None of my kin was present." You will hear that often because it is the old word for someone of very close relation to you, usually a blood relative. We added *g* onto "kin" to come up with "king." Kin, that is a relative, is one of our own people.

The word "king" carries not only the idea of kinship, but it also means noble one. A king in the Old Testament ideal was a close relative who was very noble and was promoted to rulership because of his nobility and his blood relation. Like a father as protector and head of the family, motivated by love for his family, so the king under the Old Testament concept was one who was motivated by love and related to the people, not to usurp from the outside but one who was blood relation and was very noble of character.

The King-God Concept

Some people object very strenuously to the king-god concept of the Bible, where we see God sitting on a throne high and lifted up, and that He is a great king over all the earth; where Christ is called King of kings as well as Lord of lords. But that idea runs like a golden thread through the entire Bible. Some object very strenuously, saying that the old idea of the divine right of kings dominates Scriptures, and for that reason, the whole phraseology should be changed, and the present concept of God as a king is based upon a primitive and false idea of human government. But it accords entirely with the true concept of kingliness.

A king is a noble head of his people, deriving his glory not from the servile obedience of his people but from the happiness and prosperity of his people. Read Psalm 72, where the king comes from heaven to rule over the whole earth. Read Isaiah 11, where the Lord anoints Jesus as king over the earth and you will find that the glory of king as king derives from the prosperity and freedom and happiness of His people, and that is the Old Testament concept of the king.

The whole Bible resonates with this idea. However, in human practice, it is not perfect, because rulers are men, and men are fallen. There is not anything perfect. You read in the newspapers of all these bleeding hearts that answer the question, "My husband has run away, what shall I do?" and they are always talking about a perfect marriage. You cannot have a perfect marriage because the two that make up the marriage are fallen beings. You want a perfect politician; but you will never have a perfect politician, because every politician, even if he rises to the stature of statesman, is still a fallen man. You will never have a perfect teacher or a perfect child. You will never have a perfect human, because humans are people, and people are fallen.

So the concept of rulership while it is divine, and while government is divine, will never be perfect. You will never find any form of government that is not imperfect because those who rule, whether they be in a democracy or a monarchy, are human, and humans are fallen, and fallen men are selfish, and selfish men are bad. Not all are bad. There have been noblemen, kings and queens of England, that shone as bright stars, and England looks back with nostalgic yearning to those great bold eras when noble and righteous kings ruled. The same I suppose is true in all countries.

When people were discussing politics and the right form of government in front of the famous Dr. Samuel Johnson, he cleared his throat and began with those famous words, "Sir, I perceive that it matters little what form of government prevails in a country, the people will be happy if only the rulers be righteous men." That is worthy to be written down in the halls of Congress and everywhere else throughout the world. The people will be happy if our leaders are righteous men. But they are not all righteous men, because they are humans and subject to temptation the same as everybody else.

A Reminder About Proof-texting

Peter enjoins us, in 1 Peter 2:13-16, to peaceful obedience to government, and this is to be understood by these words of Peter and by other Scriptures. Always remember that in the Bible the truth is never to be discovered by saying, "It is written," but by saying, "It is written and again it is written." Truth is never found in only one verse; truth is found in one verse plus another verse plus another verse plus another verse until the whole truth of God lies before you. If you take only one verse and make that to be supreme, and crowd out everything else, you can teach any crazy kind of doctrine in the world.

"There is no God," said a verse in the Bible, and people will, even in this day in which we live, in offices and places where people work, attack a young Christian who does not know much yet about the Bible, and say, "The Bible says there is no God." But the truth is not to be found in one verse, "there is no God." The truth is to be found in that verse plus all the other verses. And if you will read the entirety of that verse, you will find that it says, "The fool has said in his heart, there is no God" (Ps. 14:1).

Somebody might say, "I know God is a created being because He had to come from somewhere. Everybody has to come from somewhere at some time." What kind of theology is that? None of it is based upon any good, solid evidence that would hold up under scrutiny. Again, we have foolishness because they take one verse and do not add anything to it.

A Christian maid working in a home saw a nice piece of jewelry. She liked it and latched on to it. The theft was discovered, and they faced her with it. She smiled and said, "Well, I'm a Christian, and I took it because it was mine."

They said, "How do you reason that way?"

She said, "Doesn't Paul say that all things are yours?" So she figured if all things were hers, she might as well take what belonged to her. That is a misuse of Scripture. When we read, "Submit yourselves unto every ordinance of man for the Lord's sake: whether it be to the king, as supreme; or unto governors . . . for so is the will of God," we are not to take that as the end of the subject. We are to take that as being one side of a great truth—necessary, right and proper—to be obeyed but to be understood along with other truths.

For instance, Peter himself, the very man who wrote these words of our text, was one time in trouble with authorities. He had preached and prayed and the authorities took him aside: "And they called them, and commanded them not to speak at all nor teach in the name of Jesus" (Acts 4:18). Peter, undaunted by their threat, said that he would leave it to their judgment whether it was better to obey God than man (see v. 19). Then he promptly went out and began to preach. The very Peter who said, "Submit yourselves to every ordinance of man" refused to obey an ordinance of man when it conflicted with the Word of God.

It is perfectly right that I should park my car in the right place, keep traffic laws, pay income tax and keep the laws of the country. But if the laws of the country ever told me I could not pray, then as Shakespeare said of another, "It's better observed in the breech than in the observance." And by breaking a law that tells me I cannot pray, I'm a better Christian than if I kept it.

How many laws are there in our country? How many laws were there in the days of Paul that told people they could not be good? For the most part, even in the worst of countries, laws are made to keep people straight and in line, and righteous and right and as good as fallen men can be. Therefore, there is rarely a conflict between human ordinances and the laws of God, but wherever that conflict occurs, there must be disobedience.

There may come a time when only good people may be in jail. Jails were made by good people to put bad people in because the bad people were in the minority; and by putting a bad person in jail, you took him out of circulation; so the good people reluctantly made jails to put bad people in. It is conceivable that a nation can degenerate morally and politically to a point where the majority is bad. In that case, only the good people are in jail. They just take away the jails from the good people and put the good people in them. That happened in Russia, Germany and China.

When a Christian Disobeys Authority

This rule is twofold. Laws governing social relations and civil regulations are to be obeyed without question. Christians are never to be lawbreakers. They are to lead good, peaceable and law-abiding lives, and in doing that, they will silence their detractors. But the other side of that is that laws interfering with our duties to God are to be held nonobligatory by all Christians.

Daniel was in Babylon and given a high position as a good, honest, law-abiding, decent man. He served his God without breaking the laws of God while keeping the laws of Babylon. Then one day a law was passed forbidding him to pray. He broke that law without even asking whether he should. He just broke it right in the middle. He discarded one piece here and the other piece there and kept right on praying toward Jerusalem.

Of course, they put him in a den of lions; but it did not do him any harm. He came out all right. God Almighty, the King of all the kings, overruled the embarrassed king and saved Daniel.

God has not always done that. There have been martyrs by the tens of thousands who have given their lives to obey the laws of God in a society that said the laws of God were bad and forbade people to obey them.

I think we have the key here in our biblical text, and it is so simple that a wayfaring man need not err therein. "Submit yourselves to every ordinance of man for the Lord's sake: whether it be to the king, as supreme; or unto governors, as unto them that are sent by him for the punishment of evildoers, and for the praise of them that do well. For so is the will of God, that with well doing ye may put to silence the ignorance of foolish men."

So far as the laws of man do not conflict with the laws of God, a Christian's duty is to abide by the law. But as soon as they conflict with the laws of God, the Christian's duty is to be a lawbreaker instantly. The moment they tell us from Washington that we cannot preach the gospel, it will be our sacred duty to preach the gospel and go to jail. But I am glad for our country, and glad we do not have that kind of trouble.

The reason for this, of course, is that God is above all and Christ transcends all nations, all laws and all countries. Let us beware, however, in trying to nationalize Christianity. There is great danger in fusing Christianity with politics and using the gospel of Christ as a tool to political ends. May it never be so. Truth is master itself and is never to be used as a tool to an end that lies outside the truth.

There are those who use right as a means to political ends. And there are still those who so fuse and confuse Christianity with some form of government that one is made to stand for the other. It is always bad. Adolph Hitler tried to use Christianity as a tool of the state, and he went down. Joseph Stalin also tried it and went down. God Almighty, the Sovereign King, will not permit little men to make truth the tool toward selfish ends. So let us never equate Christianity with any politicalism, Americanism or any other -ism. To do so is to misunderstand Christ completely and go astray in interpretation of the whole realm of God in redemption.

The Kingdom of Christ Above All

There was democracy before Christ was born in Bethlehem or died on the cross, and there has been flourishing Christianity in lands where there was no democracy. So Christianity and democracy are not the same. Certainly, the kindly influences of the Christian gospel has softened them, raised the sense of appreciation for the individual and given us the freedom we have left in the world. And as far as Christianity is allowed to soften and touch the hearts of man, we still live in what we call the free world, but the two are not the same.

The Church rises above all governments. Jesus said, "Nation shall rise against nation, and kingdom against kingdom" in that last day (Mark 13:8). The hymn "Onward Christian Soldiers" by Sabine Baring-Gould (1834-1924) contains these words:

Crowns and thrones may perish, kingdoms rise and wane, but the church of Jesus constant will remain.

Gates of hell can never gainst that church prevail;
we have Christ's own promise, and that cannot fail.

In Matthew 25:31-33, Jesus says, "When the Son of man shall come in his glory, and all the holy angels with him, then shall he sit upon the throne of his glory: And before him shall be gathered all nations: and he shall separate them one from another, as a shepherd divideth his sheep from the goats: And he shall set the sheep on his right hand, but the goats on the left." And he will issue the words of doom and blessing, rising above all the nations, standing aloft from it all and above it all.

We happen to be pilgrims in a nation, which I, without any undue patriotic notion, believe to be the greatest nation and the best nation in the world. And we are grateful for that; but Christianity has flourished in the courts of Caesar. Christianity has flourished under the flashing sword of the heathen. Christianity is still flourishing in China; do not let them tell you it is not. It is underground, certainly, and there are still in Russia stoic old boot-wearing men of the Russian Orthodox Church who believe in God the Father Almighty and Jesus Christ His only Son, our Lord.

The gospel of Christ rises above all -isms, political views, parties and all the rest. While we are here in the middle of these swirling waters, we do the best we can to support the best political party we know and live in obedience and be good and law-abiding citizens, always knowing that we are here for only a little while; always knowing that this goodness we see about us in a political way is not Christianity. It is only something that God, in His sovereignty, has brought to pass for the last days.

God has given us all this financial prosperity in order that there might be money to evangelize in the last days. God has given all this political freedom in order that we might send missionaries in the last days. Americanism is not Christianity. The kingdom of God has no nationality. The kingdom of God has only the human race within its broad framework and the Son of man as its head and King.

We are gathered and will gather unto the new creation. "But ye are come unto mount Sion, and unto the city of the living God, the heavenly Jerusalem, and to an innumerable company of angels, to the general assembly and church of the firstborn, which are written in heaven, and to God the Judge of all, and to the spirits of just men made perfect, and to Jesus the mediator of the new covenant, and to the blood of sprinkling, that speaketh better things than that of Abel" (Heb. 12:22-24). This new creation transcends national lines, linguistic lines, racial lines and rises above it all to Mount Zion, the city of the living God.

I hope that we are properly appreciative of all of this. I hope that we are not guilty of ingratitude or even carelessness in thinking about all of this. I hope we are thankful to God for political freedom enabling us to operate without a threat of jail or death, but more thankful to God for that national line transcending race and transcending gospel to bring us into the kingdom of the new creation and make us sons and daughters of God.

12

THE CHRISTIAN
CANNOT BE HARMED

And who is he that will harm you, if ye be followers of that which is good?
1 PETER 3:13

That is a rhetorical question and a rhetorical question as you know is one that tells you the answer in itself; you do not have to answer. The answer simply is, no one. Of course, there is something about the saying in Romans 8:33-39:

> *Who* shall lay any thing to the charge of God's elect? It is God that justifieth. *Who* is he that condemneth? It is Christ that died, yea rather, that is risen again, who is even at the right hand of God, who also maketh intercession for us. *Who* shall separate us from the love of Christ? Shall tribulation, or distress, or persecution, or famine, or nakedness, or peril, or sword? As it is written, For thy sake we are killed all the day long; we are accounted as sheep for the slaughter. Nay, in all these things we are

more than conquerors through him that loved us. For I am persuaded, that neither death, nor life, nor angels, nor principalities, nor powers, nor things present, nor things to come, nor height, nor depth, nor any other creature, shall be able to separate us from the love of God, which is in Christ Jesus our Lord (emphasis added).

I emphasized the personal pronoun "who" three times in this passage in order that you might see how the Holy Spirit deals with language. He said, "Who shall lay any thing to the charge of God's elect?" "Who is he that condemneth?" "Who shall separate us?" That is a personal pronoun implying personality, but then He uses neutral things: "For I am persuaded, that neither death, nor life, nor principalities, nor powers, nor things . . ." This shows that when He says "who," He includes not only the person who might want to harm us but also things that might want to harm us. This gives me my thesis: Nothing can harm a good man, neither person nor things nor circumstances.

Defining "Harm"

Let me explain what it means to be harmed. I never like to use words I am not sure my readers understand. If I use a word meaning one thing, and you give it some other meaning, you and I might as well be talking in Chinese. So I define the word "harm" or "harmed" in my own language. I did not even look in *Webster's*; I thought this up myself, that "to harm" is "to debase in quality." That is one meaning of the word "harm."

Harm is done to gold if it could be debased by being made silver. That would be harming the gold. And if the silver could be debased by being made iron, that would be harming the silver. And if we went on we could debase the iron by making it lead; that would be debasing the iron. Then if we made the lead into clay, that would be debasing it still more. It would be a deterioration in quality that would be to harm a thing or person.

A second definition I would give is that "harm" means "to reduce in dimension or amount." An office building that has a thousand offices in it has a fire or a bombing or earthquake, and great sections, wings of the building are destroyed so that it is reduced to say 50 offices. That would be harming the building in that it would be reducing its dimensions.

Then when it comes to human beings, we would say that "harm" means "to prevent the fulfillment of our destiny." Most people do not know it, but you amount to something. God made you in His image. You have a destiny to fulfill, and harming you would mean to stymie that destiny somehow and block its fulfillment. It would mean to block the accomplishment of your appointed task. God has appointed a task for all of us, and if somehow you can be cheated out of the fulfilling of your task, you would be harmed or lowered in value. If somehow or other someone or something can get hold of me and debase me and devalue me so that I no longer signify in the eternal scheme of things as highly as I did before, but I am reduced in value, I am cheapened like devalued money, then I have been harmed.

On that definition, I can say that nothing can harm a good man or woman that follows what is good. Nothing can debase his quality, nothing can reduce his dimensions, nothing can prevent the fulfillment of his destiny, nothing can block the accomplishment of his appointed task and nothing can lower his value before God and the universe. These things cannot harm a good man. Only sin can debase us, deteriorate us; and if we deal with sin, we need to make perfectly sure that nothing else can get to us. That is, nobody can be reduced in size by anything that anybody can do to him. You cannot get any smaller.

I remember years ago the sharp-tongued Douglas McArthur said about a certain man, "He's getting smaller and smaller every day, trying to get big enough to fill his job." And you can yourself get smaller and smaller; and if you want to do it, you can debase yourself. You can reduce your size and your moral dimensions, but nobody can do it to you, and nothing nor any combination of things can reduce you.

Perspective on Earthly Harm

Think of our destiny as human beings made in the image of God. We have a higher position. I have often said that there is a morbid humility that is dishonoring to God Almighty. God made me in His image and outside of sin; I have absolutely nothing to apologize for. It is a degraded humility that crawls like a padded spaniel over the sidewalk and says, "Excuse me for living. I will die as soon as I get around to it. I'm no good; I'm nobody." That kind of thing dishonors God Almighty. "Who art thou, oh man, to speak against the potter that made thee?" The carpenter that built a house, "Who art thou to find fault with the house?"

God made you higher than the angels in that He said about you what He never said about an angel, that He made you in His own image. You have only one thing to be sorry for and ashamed of, and that is the sin that marred that image. So you have a destiny and a high moral calling as a human being; and I ask you, who can change that? Who can unmake that image in you? Who can make you anything less than God intended you to be except your own self and sin?

Then there is our appointed task. Everybody has an appointed task. I never believed in this little orphan Annie conception of all the human beings. I never believed that we were orphaned in childhood and that somehow cut loose from our moorings, that we float, driven by one wind and another, changed and twisted by all crosscurrents, and that we have no home and no beginning and no certain dwelling place. All that is deism or agnosticism, but it is not Christianity, and it is not biblical. The Bible teaches there is a sovereign God who has appointed the ways of man. It teaches that you and I are dearer to God than the apple of His eye. It teaches that God so loved the world that He gave His only begotten son. And it teaches that the very second person of the triune God came down and was made in the image of mortal flesh that He might redeem us. God did not do that for any creature that was any less than infinitely valuable. And can you imagine that anybody can take away from that value, can make you anything less than you are? You are tragically and sadly mistaken. Lowering us in value cannot be. Nobody can do it, and here we stand.

You say, "All right then, what is this, Mr. Tozer? Universalism believes that all men everywhere will be saved!"

I do not believe anything of the sort. But I believe that no external circumstance can harm me, and nobody outside me can reduce me in value nor in any way hurt me; but I believe I can hurt myself. I believe I can harm my own soul, but nobody on the outside can do it. But I can do it inside my own heart if I do not watch myself.

Can Temptation Harm Us?

I not only believe that nobody can harm me, but I also believe that nobody can harm anybody else. We use language very foolishly. One man touches another man and we say, "He did him an injury." One man starts slander about another man and we say, "He harmed that man's reputation." But we are using words very carelessly. The simple fact is that nobody can harm anybody else; all he can do is put temptation in his way and make it possible for him to harm himself.

I will give you Bible illustrations of this. You remember Adam and Eve back in the Garden of Eden. Someone will be thinking out ahead of me and say, "How do you get that way, sir? The devil harmed Adam and Eve."

I reply, "The devil did nothing of the sort." He did not harm Adam or Eve. The devil simply told Adam and Eve how they could harm themselves and they were fools enough to accept the proposition. If they had stood on their own piety and believed God, there would have been no harm done to either one of them and it would not have been said that the devil harmed them, and they would not have been harmed. But they accepted the proposition that they should harm themselves and so they harmed themselves. Unless you open the gate and let the devil in, he is totally harmless and cannot injure anybody except as he is allowed to get in.

Later on, that same devil that had succeeded in tempting the first Adam to harm himself came to the second Adam and started the same nefarious scheme. How far did he get with the second Adam? He did not get anywhere, for the second Adam did not harm Himself. The first one did, but the second one, our Lord Jesus Christ, refused to do it. And He stood on His own spirituality and His own faith and said, "It is written," and the devil went away red-faced because he had not succeeded in causing the second and last Adam to harm Himself. Jesus Christ knew better. He would not give in to temptation, and so nobody harmed Him, and the devil could not harm Him. I have never been a very devil-conscious creature. I have always been a wee bit afraid of these people who are in rapport with the dark world. I do not believe in visiting the underworld, not even for purposes of writing an article. I think we ought to stay away and out of the underworld.

That old Madame So-and-So with a rag around her head, telling fortunes in a dirty hole under the sidewalk . . . let her alone, stay away from her. What do you want to go in there for? Unless you are taking the gospel and having services, why do you want to be down in that mess? What do you want to be down there for in the first place? Why hang around with cutthroats, bums, dopers and gunmen? Stay away from them and do not be jittery and jumpy about them.

Why should we always be devil conscious? I have met people that were in such contact with the devil that he was breathing on their neck all the time and they were always praying and almost frantically praying, "O Lord, deliver me and help me." I could see that sometime during your lifetime you might have a run-in with the devil where you would have to really get down and pray. But for the most part, if you would forget about the devil and focus your attention on the eternal, everlasting, victorious Son of God, you would break the devil's heart and render him powerless.

So, nobody outside can hurt you. You go on looking over your shoulder thinking the devil is catching up with you. He will never catch up with you if your faith will believe that nothing can harm a good man.

Can Physical Injury Harm Us?

Let me point out a few things people mistakenly believe harm them. Some people imagine a physical injury harms the man, but I do not believe it. Epicurus, a Greek philosopher and stoic, had some good ideas. He said, "What's the use of worrying about external injuries and harm. I must die. Well, must I die grumbling? I must be fettered; well, must I be lamenting too? I must be exiled; well, what hinders me from going smiling and cheerful? Not even Zeus himself can get the better of my free spirit."

Those in authority threatened, "I'll throw you into prison. I'll behead that paltry body of yours." Epicurus said, "Did I ever tell you that I was the only man on earth that had a head that couldn't be taken off his body?" What can you do with a man like that? Unfortunately, Christians do not have that much sense. If we hear that somebody in Indochina or Columbia has been thrown into jail, we write a big tract about it and say, "They've been harmed."

We imagine physical injury helps or harms people. It does not. Take Abel, in the early part of the world's history. His brother did not like Abel, because Abel was a spiritual fellow, so he took him out and beat him up. It does not say how it happened, he probably did not mean to kill him, he just meant to give him a good beating, but he did not know his own strength and when he walked away, his brother was dead. So he kicked a few leaves over him, and there Abel lay, his blood crying out to God for vengeance. But was Abel harmed? Was he any less dear to God? No, he was the same great big believing Abel that he had been before, and though his poor body lay among the leaves and the dirt, he was still as great a man and as strong a man and as significant a man as he ever was.

When they stoned Stephen to death, do you think when the rocks began slamming into the ribs and head of Stephen and he finally died, did they harm Stephen? No, they did not. They injured his body, but they did not harm the man. They killed his body, but they never touched his soul. Who is he that can harm Stephen? He was a follower of that which was good. He was a man full of the Holy Ghost and wisdom; you cannot harm the Holy Ghost and you cannot harm wisdom. So Stephen was just as valuable in the scheme of things, just as wonderful and just as big as he was before they killed him.

This man we read about in the twelfth chapter of Acts, James, the man they slew with a sword, did that harm him? Not at all. The only thing it did was separate his head from his body, and he had no need for his head then anyhow. And if we only knew how little need we have of our head, we would not be so careful of the poor empty thing. Really, our heads do not amount to an awful lot. God Almighty makes us run and live by heart power. God did not say He blew in him the breath of life and he became a living head. He blew into him the breath of life and he became a living soul. In your head, God gave you the kind of steering wheel to keep you out of trouble and help you along while you are down here, but you are spirit. God made you spirit and that is the part nobody can get to. I might refer to Paul, Peter, and all the rest in their persecutions.

These early Christians wandered about in goatskins, destitute in deserts, mountains, dens and caves. Those were the persecuted ones; but the persecution came from the outside. It could not get to the inside at all. The genius of Christianity is internalism, that the kingdom of God is within you and it is inside of you. It is inside of you that you signify, and the persecutor can only get to the external. The persecutor cannot get into the mansion of your soul. He cannot get to you.

Were these persons dressed in goatskins any less valuable than the king, than Pilate dressed in his silk? No, because silk and goatskin belong to the body, whereas the value of the man lies inside of him.

Years ago, some missionaries were martyred, and it gave the printing presses, old maid poets and tear-jerking preachers ammunition for the next five years. The missionaries were killed for Christ's sake. They were not hurt at all, just made to kneel down, lean over, and they cut their heads off, but did not get to them. They did not get to the spirit of them, they never got through to the essence of them though they cut off their heads. And now they are with the Lord, and the souls of the righteous are in the hands of God, and no evil shall harm them.

I know it seems for a season that they had been injured. Actually, God had taken them away from the troubles to come. So it was a victory that they went home, not a defeat. Because we are earthbound and our faith will not penetrate the blue, we think as men think and evaluate as men evaluate, and our scale of values is that of Adam and not of God. We make a great to-do if somebody in the course of his duty dies on the battlefield of the faith. That ought to be taken in stride as a matter of course, and when a man goes, we ought to sing, "Hosanna to Jesus on high, another has entered his rest, another has escaped to the sky and is lost in Emmanuel's breast." Nobody is harmed when he is killed; nobody is injured when he dies if he is a Christian.

Can Slander Harm Us?

And then there is slander. Some people are so desperately jittery that somebody will slander them. Christ was slandered, but did it do Him any harm? They said He had a devil and a great many other terrible things about Him but it never hurt Jesus any. It never changed the love of God for His Son; it never took away the crown from the heart and head of the Savior. It never made Him any less than He was. It never closed up a single room in the mansion of His soul; it never in any wise harmed Him. Slander never hurt anybody.

Can Verbal Abuse Harm Us?

And there is abuse. This is one thing that the good of all ages have had to suffer. I suppose before Cain killed Abel, he told him off plenty. He abused him before he slew him, and all down the years the righteous have suffered abuse by the unrighteous. The twice-born had to take tongue lashing from the once-born.

Abuse has taken away a great many things from humanity but it has not taken away the power of speech. A sinner can be just as eloquent as a saint; he can be a whole lot more effective because he is more uninhibited in his use of words. When a saint starts to answer a sinner, he has to be careful and sound like a Christian. But when a sinner starts working on a saint, no holds are barred. And the names we are called are simply something lovely to behold and to hear. That sin does not take away the power of speech. The sinner can still curse and grouch, but the man of faith sees it and knows that it is simply the raven sitting on a dead limb of a blasted oak, croaking implications against the dove. The dove cannot answer because he is a dove, and so he looks modestly down at his pink feet and makes little tender noises like the dove that he is; and because he does not answer back, the raven thinks he has won the debate. But all he has done is prove that he is a raven.

If you do not get abused, God help you, you are not where you should be. If you are abused, think of that fellow abusing you as one of Adam's ravens: a fallen raven sitting on a dead limb, croaking his displeasure against the spiritual. You can afford to take it. The day will come when God will avenge all of His people, but in the meantime, the raven does not hurt you, it only gets your ear, and your ear is not you. Cursing does not get past your ear unless you let it get past your ear. Suppose the man that curses you gets you to hate him; then you have injured yourself. Suppose the man that persecutes you tempts you to malice; then you have injured yourself. Suppose you carry a sullen spirit in your breast; then you are harmed, but the devil did not do it, you did it. Keep the persecutor out of your bosom, keep hate out of your heart, keep malice out of your spirit and you are as sound as gold and nothing can harm you or get to you.

Can Physical Death Harm Us?

The last is death. We all generally agree down here among the sons of Adam that to kill a man is the last dirty trick you can do to him. Even laws based upon the fear of death say, "If you murder, we'll kill you." The fear of death is what restrains man. And we generally agree that to die is to incur the greatest damage, the greatest harm. This is Adam's philosophy, not God's. This terrible fear of death is not the teaching of the Scripture. "Precious in the sight of the LORD is the death of his saints" (Ps. 116:15).

I would not underestimate nor would I in any way try to rise poetically above death or show that death is not something to shock us and startle us and frighten us. I would be a liar if I tried it. But I believe that death is the devil's last indignity. It is the last ferocious, obscene attack he makes upon the tabernacle of the Holy Ghost. But he can only reach the tabernacle. "And fear not them which kill the body, but are not able to kill the soul: but rather fear him which is able to destroy both soul and body in hell" (Matt. 10:28). That is only the tabernacle, and the devil is not only bad, but he is dirty; and not only dirty, but obscene, hating the people of God with a hatred as old as the centuries and as black as the pit where he will go. Therefore, the devil wants to kill the people of God. He will heap all the indignities he can upon them and he will twist them, break them and make their bodies look terrible.

One of the holiest men I have ever known has been to me an outstanding example of spirituality in this degenerate hour. He has lived a long and useful life. He has been persecuted, endured a great deal of suffering, but has never so much as opened his mouth once to answer back. He is as humble as a rug, and his prayer is as lofty as an eagle, and he is a great preacher of truth.

I had not seen him for about a year. To say I was shocked when I saw him next would not be to tell all the truth. Those fiery eyes were now looking dully out through hollow sockets. A fine, rather homely but strong, good-looking face gone away to a shadow. A well-set body now bent, the arms and legs showing through the clothing like sticks, sitting looking at the floor. Death sits like a buzzard circling over him and waits, and unless God Almighty performs a miracle within the next three months, that tired, sick, holy body will be the plaything of the forces of death, and they will destroy and make it pale and gaunt and worse looking than now, and shut up the eloquent tongue and hold down the blind over those bright eyes.

Yet they'll carry away nothing. The devil will laugh and say, "I've enjoyed this indignity, this profane act of indignity against the temple that I've hated." But he has not harmed the man of God at all. And not all the devil's tricks can do it, nor the undertaker, nor the embalmer, nor the gravedigger can do it, and not the slow forces of nature that will dissolve this mortal body back to dust can harm the man, for the man was made in the image of God, redeemed by the blood of the holy Son of God and indwelt by the Holy Ghost. And so the Father, Son and Holy Ghost have made his soul their habitation, and death cannot get to that habitation. He is as young as when he was 25 years old, and he is as sound and healthy as that healthiest moment of his life, only the body is suffering, that is all.

John Adams, the second president of the United States, was getting pretty old and was emeritus elder statesman, walking around the streets of Washington. Some friend met him and said, "Mr. Adams, how are you?"

"Well," he said, "I'm all right. I never was better in my life, but my dwelling place is on mortgage and I understand they are going to foreclose before long and I'll be thrown out."

"Oh," his friend said, "how terrible for a man like you." And he started out to get money, a subscription to buy a house for this fellow. When it came back around to him, Adams laughed and said, "You misunderstood me. I was talking about this old carcass of mine. You asked how I was and I said I was all right, but there was a mortgage on my home, this old place where I've lived for these seventy so years; nature has got a mortgage and it's going to foreclose, but it hasn't bothered me any."

Now you see what I mean, don't you.

Here is my thesis. No one, no thing, no circumstance can harm a good man; and if you will believe that, you can relax. If you believe that, you can stop worrying that somebody will do you dirt. Nobody can block you, hinder your manifest destiny, reduce the size of the mansion of your soul, make you any less valuable to God or less dear to the Father. Nobody can block your ministry or stop your forward progress. Nobody can do it, nothing can do it, only you can do it. Keep sin out of your heart, walk under the blood of Christ, keep in contact with Father, Son and Holy Ghost. You can be as free as an angel that walks the streets of God, for nothing can harm a good man.

13

THE CHRISTIAN BELIEVES THE WHOLE BIBLE

For Christ also hath once suffered for sins, the just for the unjust, that
he might bring us to God, being put to death in the flesh, but quickened
by the Spirit. . . . For this cause was the gospel preached also to them
that are dead, that they might be judged according to men in the flesh,
but live according to God in the spirit.

1 Peter 3:18; 4:6

Here is a good working rule to help you rightly understand
Scripture: If you do not have more than one verse to support
what you read, do not teach it. Because, if it is not found in
more than one verse in the Bible, chances are it is not found
there either, and what you think is a passage teaching a certain
thing does not teach it at all.

Suppose that I was going to argue for the future life, and I
would write to people who practice baptism for the dead and

say to them, "How could you deny the future life when you practice baptism for the dead?" I would be saying, in effect, "Now you yourself have made a future life because you are acting as though those persons who had died were still in existence. Therefore, you believe in a future life and your very practice of baptism for the dead proves it." That would not mean I approved baptism for the dead; it would only show that I was arguing that they believed in a future life by the fact that they are attempting to help people in the future life.

Paul asked the question, "Else what shall they do which are baptized for the dead, if the dead rise not at all? Why are they then baptized for the dead?" (1 Cor. 15:29). That did not mean he approved this practice, for he did not in any way practice baptism for the dead, nor did he exhort anybody to do it, nor is there one line in the Bible that teaches it. But he appeals to something that some of them at least did and believed in to show how inconsistent they were in saying there is no bodily resurrection. And it is obvious that the same people who said there was no resurrection were the same ones who practiced baptism for the dead.

Then take that famous passage, "And I will give unto thee the keys of the kingdom of heaven: and whatsoever thou shalt bind on earth shall be bound in heaven: and whatsoever thou shalt loose on earth shall be loosed in heaven" (Matt. 16:19). Now that is obviously an obscure passage. I have never heard it satisfactorily explained.

Some will deny that the Bible has any authority over the church on the grounds that the Bible came out of the church and not the church out of the Bible. They will deny whole sections of

Scripture because they say, "You don't understand it, and besides that, it isn't binding upon us because the Bible is a daughter of the church and not the church a daughter of the Bible; therefore, the Bible has no authority over the church." But if you complain that the pope is not Christ's vice-regent on earth, they will run to that obscure passage, "I will give unto thee the keys of the kingdom." They say, "How dare you deny the Bible, for the Bible says 'I will give unto you the keys of the kingdom,' and that was Peter; and the pope is the descendant of Peter."

Obscure Scripture Often Attracts False Teaching

I do not know how we get that way, but false teaching always hunts an obscure passage. That reminds me of the Mormon missionary traveling, and somebody says to him, "You believe in a variety of wives. How do you deal with that passage that says, 'Let the bishop be the husband of one wife'?" He replies, "That means at least one." He explained it anyhow.

A heresy always hunts obscurity, and false teaching always hunts the difficult text. You see, it is as if I were to take you to my farm and say to you, "Here you will find apples and peaches and grapes and watermelons and cantaloupes and sweet pota-toes," and I would name 15 or 20 edible fruits or vegetables or grains and say, "Now, this is all yours, take over." Then I came back a month later and found my guests half starved, and said to them, "What's the matter? You look undernourished."

They would say, "We are undernourished because we have found a plant that we cannot identify. There is a plant behind the old oak stump back there in the near end of the far field, just over the hill, and we have stayed one month trying to identify this plant."

"But you're starving! You've got so many other plants around you, but you look sick. What's the matter with you?"

And they would reply, "We're worried about this one plant."

That is exactly what many of God's children do. They starve themselves to death knee-deep in clover because there is one little old plant back of the stump in the rear end of the field that they cannot identify. Heretics are always starving to death while they worry about that one obscure passage of Scripture. I am not going to leave out this passage in 1 Peter in order that nobody will come and worry you with it and say that they know what it means and therefore try to prove that you are wrong.

Read the Text Rightly

First, what does this verse *not* teach? It does not teach universalism. Universalism is the belief in the restitution of all fallen beings to a state of blessedness. Some of them believe only in the restoration of all human beings to blessedness, and that not only Christians but also all human beings go finally to blessedness. Then there is another kind of moral exhaustive universalism, which teaches not only the restitution of all human beings but also restitution of the devil and all the fallen angels. They are very generous and take in everything—every human and every creature that is fallen and has sinned against God.

This universalism teaching that every moral creature would finally be saved is a dream born of desire and springs from humanitarian motives, no doubt. Humanitarian feelings will at best lead us to desire the salvation of all, but it does not talk of the Scriptures. The Bible specifically states, "Except ye repent ye shall all likewise perish." It pictures a hell where the devil and all his angels are, and everyone not found in the Book of Life are finally consigned there. So the teaching of the Bible is definitely not universalism, and whatever this passage teaches it does not teach universalism.

Second, it does not teach a second chance. The Russellites—I do not call them Jehovah's Witnesses because I do not want to soil that holy name identifying it with any false teachers—teach that there is a second chance. They say that those who die will have a chance in the future world, and if he turns down that chance, he will be annihilated, he will cease to be. When a sinner dies, he sleeps in the earth, body and soul in a state of deep unconsciousness; and then when the resurrection comes, he will be raised and given another chance. If he turns down that chance, then he will be annihilated and cease to be and there will be no hell. That is what the Russellites teach.

Of course, this error thrives on a difficult text. It cannot stand the full bright light of the Bible; it cannot stand the teachings of Jesus; it cannot stand the book of Romans, the book of Hebrews, the book of Revelation, and it cannot stand the four Gospels. This heresy cannot possibly stand up under all the light of the Bible. It is a nice blooming plant and blooms in the shadow of the human thought; but as soon as we turn the whole Bible loose on it, it withers and dies.

Lost Souls

What does "the gospel preached also to them that are dead" mean? It means that there are lost souls. The Scriptures call it "spirits in prison" and "them that are dead." And some of these in the passage are identified as being the earth's population at the time of Noah's flood. They heard the message preached and they denied or refused it, they rejected it, and the result was that they perished along with their evil deeds at the coming of the Flood. And it teaches us that these all went to the place of the dead—Hades in the New Testament, Sheol in the Old. And Christ's body, when He died, lay three days in Joseph's new tomb, but His spirit was not in His body, but separated temporarily from His body, and in that spirit He then preached to the spirits that were in Hades, the spirits in prison.

The Apostle's Creed says this about our Lord: "Who was conceived by the Holy Ghost, born of the virgin Mary, suffered under Pontius Pilate, was crucified, dead, and buried; He descended into hell. The third day He arose again from the dead. . . ."

That is only saying what Peter and Paul said. When Jesus Christ's spirit was freed from the crucified body, it did not lie quiescent or hover over the tomb. Jesus Christ the Eternal Son, in His spirit, had a work to do. The work He had to do was to go, descend into hell, that is, descend not into the fires of hell for punishment, but descend to the place of the dead and there preach the Word to those that had died and whose spirits were confined there. And so He preached the soundness of Noah's position and He told them why judgment had come and He justified the ways of God to man and explained what had taken place in order that they might know that they were being treated as intelligent beings.

God treats every human being as an intelligent being. You may not be as smart as Einstein, but you are morally intelligent and God will never violate your intelligence. He never means that you could simply shut your eyes and gulp and swallow whatever is given to you. He means that you are an intelligent moral being and therefore He will not violate your intelligence nor will He treat you like a moron.

In an ordinary American court of law, something like this goes on: Evidence is heard, the jury goes out and deliberates, they come back in, and then they pronounce the defendant guilty. The judge says, "Will the defendant please rise and face the court." The defendant rises and the judge says something to this effect: "Mr. So-and-So, the evidence has been heard and the jury of your peers has decided from the evidence that you have been guilty of such and such a crime. Before you are sentenced is there anything you want to say?" In other words, "We're about to sentence you, but we're not abnegating your intelligence, we're not treating you like a robot. You are an intelligent human being, and you're able to judge us; and if we as a judge and jury are wrong, you judge us. Therefore, I want to clear this whole matter up. Have you anything to say?"

Usually the defendant does not, but if there is anything to say in his defense, this intelligent sinner could say it to the judge, and the judge would give it respectful consideration; for American courts are not going to railroad a man to the electric chair or to prison. They are going to do it according to the rules of justice, with all the jury there and all the process open before the eyes of mankind.

So God says that all the wicked were sucked away by a flood and hurled to the place of the dead, and they will never see the blessedness of heaven or know God. But we are not simply going to seek them. They are human, they are intelligent, they are moral creatures, they are capable of exercising judgment on their own life; and therefore, the everlasting Son of God went before the spirits in prison and preached to them there. He preached to them because they were alive in their spirit; they had sinned in the flesh and they were to be judged for the days they lived in the flesh.

It you do not believe this, let me give you some Scripture to show why Christ descended into the place of the dead, why He descended into hell. Ephesians 4:8-10, says, "Wherefore he saith, When Christ ascended up on high, he led captivity captive, and gave gifts unto men. (Now that he ascended, what is it but that he also first descended into the lower parts of the earth? He that descended is the same also that ascended up far above all heavens, that he might fill all things.)"

When Jesus Christ's body lay in the grave, His spirit went to those captives in the place of the dead, and He preached release to them. When He rose, He took with Him all the redeemed spirits of ransomed men that had been trapped in the place of the dead, in Hades. Remember, Jacob said that he would go down into the grave—down unto Sheol, Hades—mourning for his son (see Gen. 37:35). When Samuel, the dead man, came back from the dead, he came up out of the earth (see 1 Sam. 28:13); but after Christ had taken the redeemed ones with Him to heaven, to the place of Paradise, Paul said that He was caught up into paradise, into the third heaven (see 2 Cor. 12:2,4)—no longer down, but up.

The Lord Himself, the Lord of life and glory, has taken His ransomed ones out of the place of the dead. That place of the dead contained not only redeemed ones but also the ones that were not redeemed, separated however by a gulf, a great gulf that was fixed. Lazarus and the rich man explained that. When the rich man died, he went to the place of the dead. When Lazarus died, he went to the place of the dead, but this time to Abraham's bosom, with a great gulf fixed between. So when our Lord descended after His death, He descended into Hades, took all of Abraham's bosom with Him up to heaven and left the rest there; but in doing it He explained it and preached in His spirit to all those that were in the place of the dead.

If that isn't enough, let me give you Philippians 2:9-11: "Wherefore God also hath highly exalted [Jesus], and given him a name which is above every name: that at the name of Jesus every knee should bow, of things in heaven, and things in earth, and things under the earth; and that every tongue should confess that Jesus Christ is Lord, to the glory of God the Father." So that not only those in heaven and those on earth, but those in hell are forced to confess with their tongue that Jesus Christ is Lord; and this they did for the glory of God the Father.

True and Righteous Judgment

Peter does not teach universalism, only that Jesus Christ our Lord, while His body lay in the grave, went in the spirit to Sheol, the place of the dead. There He preached deliverance to the ransomed and judgment to the lost, took His ransomed beings with Him, and left the lost for the judgment of the Great Day. But everyone who is under the earth and lives on the earth and all creatures everywhere admit that Jesus Christ is Lord, to the glory of God the Father.

This Jesus Christ our Lord is not going to rule over any that do not readily submit to His rule. He will not enforce His rule over one human being or one moral creature. But He will force on the unwilling tongues of even lost ones the fact that He is right. "Lord God Almighty, true and righteous are thy judgments" (Rev. 16:7) will be the only text in hell. I am not sure it will not be cognizance of that terrible place. In order that that might be known through all the worlds above, and on the earth, and beneath the earth, there had to be a declaration of the whole just plan of God to those that are dead as well as those that live.

But there is not one sentence, not one phrase, not one word, not one letter in the Bible that teaches that Jesus ever preached the gospel to the dead and said, "Come unto Me." He said, "Come unto Me" to the living. He preached the gospel of redemption and gave an invitation and said, "It is appointed unto men once to die, but after this the judgment" (Heb. 9:27). Preaching to the dead was done in order that the dead, as well as the living—the lost as well as the saved—might know how true and just and righteous our God is and how impeccable is His character, how holy are His ways, and He does all things well.

14

THE CHRISTIAN IS A STRANGER IN A STRANGE LAND

Forasmuch then as Christ hath suffered for us in the flesh, arm your-
selves likewise with the same mind: for he that hath suffered in the flesh
hath ceased from sin; that he no longer should live the rest of his time in
the flesh to the lusts of men, but to the will of God. For the time past of
our life may suffice us to have wrought the will of the Gentiles, when
we walked in lasciviousness, lusts, excess of wine, revellings, banquet-
ings, and abominable idolatries: Wherein they think it strange that ye
run not with them to the same excess of riot, speaking evil of you: Who
shall give account to him that is ready to judge the quick and the dead.

1 PETER 4:1-5

According to Peter, a Christian is one who has fled for refuge to Christ. He has identified himself with Christ and has received life from Christ. That, essentially, is what it means to believe on Jesus Christ. The Scriptures use three prepositions: "*to* Christ," "*with* Christ" and "*from* Christ."

Cowardice does not make us flee for refuge when we are in grave peril. Suppose a man were in 50-degree below zero weather and knew there was shelter in close proximity. However, he refused to go there and stayed where he was, only to freeze to death. That would be moral recklessness amounting to insanity. The same would be true for a moral being in a moral universe who knows that his sins have imperiled him forever and learns that there is in the Rock of Ages a refuge for sinners but does not avail himself of that refuge. He is not a brave man who refuses that refuge; he is a moral fool.

I do not hesitate to say that a Christian is one who has fled for refuge to Jesus Christ. Having fled to Christ, he has identified himself with Christ completely. His identification has become such that wherever Christ is he wants to be. Whatever Christ stands for, he wants to stand for. Whatever Christ is against, he wants to be against. Whoever is Christ's friend, he wants to be his friend. Christ's enemies, he is willing to have as his enemies too. The work that Christ is interested in, he wants to do. What Christ is not interested in, he takes very lightly and gives little attention to. He has identified himself with Christ, and Christ has given him life for this—spiritual life. "I give unto [him] eternal life; and [he] shall never perish, neither shall any man pluck [him] out of my hand" (John 10:28), and thus he has life. He has received life from Christ; he has identified himself with Christ and has fled for refuge to Christ.

Time Past and Time Future

Two phrases are used here, and both have the word "time" in them. "The time past" and "the rest of his time." The time past of our life may suffice us to have walked in lasciviousness, lusts, drinking, reveling, banqueting and idolatries. I think there is a bit of irony here. Peter is saying, "Haven't you had enough of these things?" He is not giving us a rundown on all that we did; he is simply giving us some samples of the way we lived and the way the people of the world live now (all the people of the world, for all have sinned). These are not taken by any means to include everything a sinner did, does or used to do; but he simply gives a sample—lasciviousness and drinking and reveling and banqueting and idolatries touch all phases of our social and religious lives.

So Peter is basically saying, "In time past you lived like that, but it can end now because God makes all things new." Let us repent of our sins and let us be very sorry for them, but let us not be discouraged by them. Let us not in any way permit them to discourage us from believing, for God is the one who makes all things new, and this embraces the land of beginning again. You had a bad beginning and you went on in a bad way, but at any time you choose, you may begin another kind of life and call that life that is past, a time past.

Second, "the rest of his time." We all know the time past of our lives. Everybody knows how old they are and sometimes they count them on their fingers. I asked a cute little girl one time how old she was, and she held up four fingers and said, "Three." Your time past—how long has it been? Your time past may have been 10 years, 21, 43, 70—whatever the number of years, you know your time past.

But how many could tell what the rest of his time will be? You know what the time past has been, but what is the time yet before you? I wonder, can you guarantee one year? Could you guarantee that you will still be here two years from now? What is the rest of your time? We all celebrate our time past, and people bring us gifts reminding us that we have had another birthday. That is the time past, but what is the rest of our time? Has anybody given you any present celebrating the rest of your time? What a foolish thing to do. Nobody knows whether he will have another birthday. Is there one who would stand up and say, "I will bet on the next three months; I am sure of the next two months"? Is there anyone here who could say, "I am sure of the next month"? Nobody knows.

A friend of mine that I have known for more than 25 years went to the doctor with a complaint. The doctor said it was indigestion and advised him to take it easy. He agreed, and so he went home, went to bed that night, got up the next morning and before he could get dressed tumbled over on the floor and was dead. He did not expect that. He fully believed he had a long time yet to live. If anyone had said to him the night before, "Brother Collette, what is the rest of your time?" He would have replied, "Well, I've got a meeting I want to hold in thus and thus town; then I want to take in this convention and be a Bible teacher there." However, he did not have much "rest of his time."

The Bible says, "The time past he lived a certain way, but the rest of his time he lives to the will of God." Thomas à Kempis said, "Oh, how wise and happy is he that laboreth to be such a one in his life as he will desire to be found at the hour of his death." It says that for the rest of your time you are not going to live the way you did for the time past. Therefore, "They think it strange," that vague pronoun without any urgency, "they think it strange." Who are "they"? It is a technical word meaning worldly people who are not renewed, who have not fled for refuge to Christ, who have not identified themselves with Christ and who have not received life from Christ. They, whoever they may be, rich or poor, old or young, far and near, think it strange that you run not with them as you used to do.

A New Life

That is another characteristic, a lesser characteristic, but it is truly a characteristic of a Christian: he is one who no longer runs with them. Doing this has ruined many a beginner. There have been those who have gone into the prayer room and, on their knees, tearfully told God that they were tired of the past and wanted to be a Christian. Then they have got up and gone out to run with the people they used to run with, and the result has been tragedy and failure in that Christian life—tragedy and failure in the Christian life because we have run with those that we should not have run with. "If ye run not with them, they think it very strange."

Worldly friends know only one life—the life they now live—and feel that to leave that life would be to die. But the Christian has found another life, more real, more exciting, more satisfying than the life he had before, and he is living that life to the will of God. The sinner does not know this; he only thinks there is one kind of life and only one life. It is not uncommon for a young person who is trying to follow the Lord, to hear this said about him, "What does he do? What kind of life does he live? Oh, how dead that is, how meaningless that is. There's no fun in that." That is the common approach to the Christian by the world; they think it strange because they are not informed that there is another life.

The disciples in their imperfection came to our Lord Jesus and said, "Master, we have brought you meat and bread." At the time, He was sitting on the edge of a well in Samaria; the woman at the well had been talking with Him and He with her (see John 4). The disciples said, "How do you have anything to eat, nobody having brought you anything?" Jesus said, "I have meat to eat that ye know not of." They thought He had not eaten because He had not eaten the food they were used to. But He said, "I recognize another kind of food and another kind of life and I have been living and eating My Father's food and giving help to the needy, and that is life to Me."

It has been true with the Christian since that time. People constantly come against him, not understanding him and marking him off as being dead because he no longer lives the kind of life he used to live or runs with them to the same excess of living or dying. So the Christian is considered strange.

What Makes Something Strange?

Let me toss that word "strange" around a little bit. The word "strange" comes from the same word we get our word "stranger." Of course, a stranger is someone not integrated in the landscape, someone that is not socially a part of the group. He is a newcomer. Out in the Old West they commonly greeted each other, "Good morning, stranger." A stranger was someone that was strange. His clothes were strange, his face was strange, maybe even his language was strange; and if you get different enough from people, you get to a point of becoming an object of their laughter.

Dr. Max I. Reich, that great Jewish saint that taught at Moody Bible Institute, wore a little beard. He told me rather ruefully that he used to have to take a good deal of abuse from boys and girls on the street who would look at his beard, then look at each other and smile. He was strange because he had a beard.

If we were as natural as we ought to be, we would be strange without a beard, because nature put a beard on the front of the average person's face, but we cut it off. But if anybody leaves it on, we say, "He is strange." Isn't that strange that we mutilate nature and say, "That's natural," and then if nature just has its way, we say, "That's strange"? When a boy in the Navy or somewhere in the service, just for the fun of it, sends home a picture of himself with a two weeks' worth of beard, everybody roars with good-natured laughter. It does not look like the boy that went into the service, so well-groomed and carefully looked after. He has been out on a trip, and so he let his beard grow. I have seen pictures like that and then they do not even look like themselves; they look strange when actually they only look natural. In reality, they look strange after they get through cutting off their beard.

Anything is strange when it is not like the rest of the things around it. Toss a German down in the midst of an English-speaking people and his accent immediately marks him. He is strange because his tongue is a little thicker and his voice a little further down than the American. Take a Frenchman whose voice is in his nose and he is different because he talks up in his nose; you have to have adenoids to speak French. He is strange because he sounds a little different from what we are used to.

So, a Christian is considered strange. I am not going to waste any tears on anybody who comes whimpering to me for sympathy because people think he is strange for following Christ. In public school, where they read the Bible, a teacher reads a few verses and maybe they say the Lord's Prayer together. Some little fellow's parents, who are atheists, scandalize the school board and say, "We want to enter an official protest. It embarrasses our little boy when they read Scripture. He is taught at home that Scripture is not true and he is embarrassed when they all bow their heads and say the Lord's Prayer; he does not believe in the Lord's Prayer. They think he is strange. We want to offer a protest." What kind of cowards are they anyhow?

Christian parents know that their children go to grade school and then high school marked as being odd, and you make no protest. Christians know there is no use to make a protest; of course, they think we are strange, but strange means different, that is all. Of course we are different; and woe be to the Christian that is not. The moment that it cannot be said of the Christian that he is different is the day he has disgraced his testimony and sold out his fate. It is the mark of a church that they are people that are different. They think it is strange that you are different, but, says Peter, "Don't put in a protest, hire a lawyer, scandalize anybody, approach the school board. They shall give account to God." There is his answer. Those who think we are strange and insist upon saying so with much laughter shall give an account to God and not to the Christian. God never made me a judge over anybody, and He never made you a judge. He made us witnesses, but not judges.

A Good Kind of Strangeness

Never call your critics to account. Explain to them if you can, but if they will not accept the explanation, fall silent. Silence is the most eloquent answer to some critics. We have the example of our Savior, for when they were questioning Him, abusing Him, He was silent, and Pilate said, "Why don't you speak to me? Don't you know that I have the power to release you or the power to crucify you?" Then Jesus spoke and said, "Thou couldest have no power at all against me, except it were given thee from above" (John 19:11). And then He fell silent. And the silence of the Lamb has been one of the wonders of the centuries. He was led as a sheep to the slaughter, and as a Lamb, He was without speech. Never try to call your critics to account. Silence is always and often the best.

We take this example from Christ, "forasmuch then as Christ hath suffered for us in the flesh, arm yourselves likewise with the same mind: for he that hath suffered in the flesh hath ceased from sin" (1 Pet. 4:1). Sure, we are different. If we are not different, woe be to us in the day of Christ. Of course we are strange, and being strange they will think us strange, but being strange only because we are morally cleaner than somebody else is not anything to disgrace us.

Some Christians, in association with their work, attend banquet functions where everybody is drinking alcohol. They drink water and grape juice and are thought to be strange because they do not indulge. However, when somebody gets into trouble, who do they come to for prayer? They come to the strange fellow who will not drink liquor.

Some work in offices where their mouth is the only clean mouth in the office; the rest of them are borderline or outright dirty. You have the only clean mouth, so they ride you by telling off-color jokes to try to stir you; but you do not laugh and you do not go along with it. You are strange to them. A clean thing is always strange when passed down in the middle of dirty things. A clean mouth is always a strange mouth when it is surrounded by unclean mouths. A pure heart is strange when it is surrounded by impure hearts.

An honest man is strange when in the midst of dishonest men, but it is a good kind of strangeness. The church of Jesus Christ should be different because she is clean-mouthed, honest and pure-minded. But the world thinks it strange that you run not with them. But don't you try to ride them for it now, because they are going to give account to God who is able to judge the quick and the dead. You are a witness but not a judge, and Christ is your example. He suffered and kept still. You and I can afford to do the same, and really, I do not think it is too serious myself, I do not think it is too serious.

Let a sinner go long enough and far enough and he will become strange the other way. When a man becomes a rapist or a murderer or bank robber, he is strange, too, and the world puts him in jail as being different, strange and dangerous; but he is different over on the other side. A Christian is different on the right side. Hello, stranger, God bless you. The stranger you are, the better you will be. We Christians who have fled for refuge to Jesus have identified ourselves with Jesus and have received life from Jesus.

15

THE CHRISTIAN BEARS HIS SUFFERING WITH JOY

Beloved, think it not strange concerning the fiery trial which is to try you, as though some strange thing happened unto you: But rejoice, inasmuch as ye are partakers of Christ's sufferings; that, when his glory shall be revealed, ye may be glad also with exceeding joy.

1 PETER 4:12-13

Adversity is the companion to every Christian on his way to Paradise. The more difficult the path, the more joy for him who follows his Lord. The Christian can bear adversity better if we can get three things straight.

First, if we can *identify* them. Strange evils are always more terrifying. We are always afraid of that which we cannot identify. If we do not know what it is, we are scared. That is human nature, and I suppose it is not anything for us to worry about or imagine we need to see a psychiatrist. It is just our human nature that half the victory is won over fear when we know what it is. When we can identify the object of our fear, when we know what it is that is troubling us, much of the trouble disappears. I might add that that is one of the basic tenets upon which psychiatry is established, and they are right as far as that goes. If you can identify your troubles, you have them half whipped. When Peter said, "Think it not strange," he was identifying their troubles for them and pointing out that these were not strange but familiar, and these persons were suffering along with all the rest.

The second thing to help us bear adversity is when we *expect* them. Unexpected blows are always the ones that do the deadliest work. When we expect a blow, we can brace against it both physically and psychologically; but a blow that comes out of nowhere is the one that does the greatest harm.

The third thing is that we know that the adversities are *common* to all. A lovable, if curious, twist in human nature is that if we know everybody else is as bad off as we are, it makes it easier for us to be bad off.

I cannot explain that. I only know that it works that way. Suppose you are cut off from all the people in the Chicago area and subjected to three weeks of some frightfully overbearing heat. If you knew that everybody else in the city of Chicago, from the greatest to the least, was comfortable, relaxed and going about in comfortable clothes, that knowledge would step up the intensity of your suffering very greatly. But there is something half-humorous and comforting in the knowledge that if you are sweating, everybody else is too. And if you have to go out and face the hot breath of nature, everybody else does too. And even if they are in an air-conditioned office, you know they will step out on the street and nearly fall over from the heat, and somehow you get a restful feeling that you are not alone in this. That is neither a divine thing nor a spiritual thing, just a natural thing.

Some things are natural but bad. That is, they stem out of an evil disposition, which is natural but bad. Then there are things that stem out of nature itself and are not tainted particularly like this. These things are a part of human nature. They are neither to be apologized for nor repented of. Does it comfort you to know that you are only one of 4 million other suffering people? Does that bother you? Just take what you can out of it when it gets hot. Remember, there are three things that God takes account of in human life: those things that are natural and good; those things that are natural but bad; and those things that are spiritual.

Peter identified the fiery trials for them, and this cooled the fire of the furnace very greatly. He said, "Beloved, think it not strange concerning the fiery trial which is to try you, as though some strange thing happened unto you" (1 Pet. 4:12). No, what's happening to you is not strange; it is familiar and a part of the pattern of life unto the Son. Then he said, "Rejoice ye." They are told here to rejoice that they are given a part in the pains of Christ.

This knowledge took the rest of the fire out of their suffering. They knew that they were not only suffering familiar sufferings, but their adversaries were familiar adversaries known to all people since time began. They were given the high privilege of suffering and bearing the pains of Christ. These first Christians were uncritically simple. The complicated reasoning with which we overcast everything now and the pale cast of fog that takes away the simplicity of our living were not known to them.

Those first Christians trusted the sufferings of Christ and related their sufferings to His. Christ was the great sufferer, they testified, and when we suffer for His sake, we are relating our suffering to Him and bearing His suffering alone with Him. Then they related their reward to His. Peter said that plainly here: "Rejoice, inasmuch as ye are partakers of Christ's sufferings; that, when his glory shall be revealed, ye may be glad also with exceeding joy" (1 Pet. 4:13). Therefore, they rejoiced in the great honor that was done them in being permitted to suffer for Christ's sake and thus endure the pains of the Lord Jesus after Him.

Reproached for the Name of Christ

Then Peter said, "If ye be reproached for the name of Christ" (1 Pet. 4:14). It is hard for modern man to understand this, but imagine, if you will, a man whose person was wonderful, a man around whose head clustered miracles, healings, deliverances, kind deeds, forgiving words, consolations and encouragement, a man who shone like the sun on men, a man who fell like the gentle rain on the hearts of men, who breathed on men and made them strong again. This man's bold claim was that He was the one whom the world had long expected, the one the ancient prophets talked about. He was the one who was adored by children, outcasts, honest men and serious women and yet was hated by organized religion.

Institutionalized religion could not find a place for Christ. He was the stone that did not fit into the building. They had all the stones they wanted, and when the chief cornerstone appeared, the architects could not find a place to fit this stone, so they rejected Him as being useless. Finally, they executed Him by trickery, sent Him out to die on a cross. And worst of all for them, it was claimed that many had seen Him alive and that this criminal that had been put to death was not dead anymore but was now alive and was more at the head of His followers than He had been before.

Can you imagine the violent effect that that name "Christian" would have? That name would have not only reasonable meaning but also have violent, emotional, explosive power. Every man stood to be counted; he was either for Christ or against Him. You reverently worshiped Him, believed that He was God indeed, and knelt in quiet worship, for the clusters of healing and health, consolation, peace and rehabilitation were round the head of Jesus. Or, they accepted the beliefs of organized religion, claimed He was a mad man filled with the devil and was out to destroy organized society. There could be no neutrality there. They had to get on one side or the other.

In our smoothed-over age, it is not so violent, not so sharp; men are not so lined up as they were then, because they are not so simple, not so direct, not so human. In this age of plastic, men are not so simple, and yet it was this simplicity that Jesus Christ praised above all human virtues when He said, "Except ye be converted, and become as little children" (Matt. 18:3). It was the simplicity of childhood, not the ignorance of childhood, not the dirt of childhood, not the noise of childhood, but the simplicity of it.

Little children have many qualities we pray they will outgrow as fast as they can. But the one thing we do not want them to outgrow, but yet grievously we see them outgrow, is simplicity. That direct immediacy belongs to the unspoiled human breast. So, the early Christians got on one side or the other, and His detractors flared into fury at the mention of His name, and His followers bowed their heads and said, "My Lord and my God." That was the division, the sharp cleavage, and it has existed wherever the church has been pure. It has existed wherever men have put away their half-knowledge and have come like children to look into the face of God.

"Let none of you suffer as . . . an evildoer" (1 Pet. 4:15). Here we see the salty practicality of the Christian way. The Christian faith is not immunity for wrongdoers. It has often done it, we admit that, but according to the Bible, it is never to be so. If you suffer, remember, it is not a strange thing but easy to understand, and your Lord went that way before you. But if any of you are being reproached for wrongdoing, do not hide behind your Christian immunity. The deacon who does not pay his bills, the pastor who leaves the city owing debts, he cannot— he dare not—hide these evils behind clerical immunity or Christian immunity. Peter says, "Let nobody suffer as . . . an evildoer." To use the faith of Christ to hide evil is to prove ourselves false and bring down judgment on our own heads; and judgment must begin at the house of God.

This is a club often used against Christians: "Judgment must begin at the house of God" (1 Pet. 4:17). People shrug their shoulders, toss their noses in the air and turn away from the Church and say, "Let judgment begin at the house of God," or, more simply, "Sweep your own doorsteps first." But I wonder if they read the rest of that verse: "For the time is come that judgment must begin at the house of God: and if it first begin at us, what shall the end be of them that obey not the gospel of God?"

One thing God will not permit is an outsider's interference in His family affairs. He will not allow the outsider to quote or misquote garbled or emasculated Scriptures; He will not allow them to use a club over the head of His child. He said, "Judgment must begin at the house of God," and the angry unbeliever said, "Yes, judgment must begin with you; why don't you mind your own business?" Then God adds, "But if it begin among My own children, how terrible it will be for those who did not even care to become My children." The ungodly and the sinner, where shall they appear? This is one of those dramatic, rhetorical questions that has no answer and that carries its own answer in it. Where shall they appear, the "ungodly shall not stand in the judgment, nor sinners in the congregation of the righteous" (Ps. 1:5)?

David said it centuries before, and now Peter repeats it almost word for word. "Wherefore let them that suffer according to the will of God commit to the keeping of their souls in well doing, as unto a faithful Creator" (1 Pet. 4:19). Whatever kind of suffering that may be, if you suffer out of the will of God, you have no reward, no encouragement from heaven or earth. If you suffer according to the will of God, we are told plainly what to do—commit your soul in well-doing unto a faithful Creator.

The Committal of Your Soul

I love words, and I love to unwrap them to find out what they contain. Sometimes in unwrapping a little further, you will find a buried treasure you did not know was there. "Commit," it says here. It means to deposit for protection.

A Deposit

A man rents a safe deposit box and puts in it deeds, insurance policies and things he wants to keep. He puts them there for protection, knowing that by and large they are safer there in a bank surrounded by guards and with steel gates and all the rest. They are safer there than they would be in his bedroom or in a cookie jar. He puts them where he thinks they are safe; he commits them. He deposits them for protection. And so Peter says, "Your sufferings are not strange, they are familiar, everybody has had to endure them; and if you are suffering in the will of God, why turn your soul over to God for protection? Deposit it; make a deposit of your soul."

Deposit means to take your hand off the thing. Some people love their money so much that they will not give it up. They want to count it when the lights are low, the window blinds are tight and the doors are locked. They want to take it out and see it; they cannot deposit it because they feel that if they do not keep bodily contact with it, it is not safe. They do not realize that it is safer away from them than it is with them. But that is the peculiarity of people; so sometimes we must deposit our souls. We must turn them over to God.

I like to think that my committal to God is similar to the mailing of a letter. You take a letter, slip it in a mailbox and hold on to it, pull it back to see if it is stamped and addressed correctly, and then give it that last minute look; but you still have your letter. Uncle Sam cannot touch it, not all the police in America dare lay a finger on that letter. The president of the United States could not, under the law, take that letter out of your hand. Nobody can take that letter from you. That is your letter, and as long as you hold it, it is yours to do with as you please. You wrote it, you addressed it, you stamped it, you sealed it, you carried it there to the corner; and if you put it back in your pocket, you still have your letter. But if you want to deposit it, you have to let loose of it. Put it in the box, reach through the slot and then let go; and until you have let go you have not made your deposit. When you let go, then you do not dare touch it, and any cop in the city can arrest you if you do touch it. After you drop it in, Uncle Sam has it. His big star-spangled hand closes on your letter and you are through with it. And if you reach your arm in there, if it were possible, and pull out that letter, you could be arrested. Committal means committal. It means depositing for protection.

A Transfer

It also means something else. It means to deliver to another's charge and to mark an absolute transfer, make an absolute transfer to superior power. So Peter says, "Make a transfer of your soul to a superior power. Turn yourself over to God." Have you done that? If you have not, then I do not know that I have much consolation for you, because you are a victim of the ebbing slow circumstances. You are a victim of every new seer that comes on the horizon. You are a victim of luck and chance and happenstance and perchance and possibility, enemies known and unknown, the latest germ that slips in. You are a victim of all uncertainty of the world if you have not made that deposit. But if you have made that deposit, you are victim of none of these things. Nobody ever worries about a letter he dropped in the mailbox; it will get there all right.

For years, I have sent packets, letters, packages, airmail, special delivery and I have never lost one. And there has never been one sent me that I know about that ever has been lost; it always gets there. The United States Post Office is trustworthy when it comes to the mail. It may be a little slow, a little expensive, but he will get it there. So you commit your soul and well-doing unto a superior power, and then you will not have to worry about yourself.

That is the only true peace I know and the only way I know to find peace. If I tell you death is not real, I am lying to you. If I tell you there are no enemies, I am lying to you again. If I tell you that you have absolute assurance of so many years ahead for you, I am lying some more. If I tell you that pain is not real, it is only thought to be so, you know I am not telling the truth. But if I tell you that pain is real, adversaries are real, but I know where you can put yourself, like a document in a safe deposit vault, I am telling you the place where nobody can get to you, where you are as safe as the character of the bank that holds you.

This is not a bank this time, but Almighty God called the Faithful Creator. Turn yourself over to your Faithful Creator through Jesus Christ. Put yourself into His hands by one final act of your soul. Say, "Lord, suffering or rejoicing, whatever the circumstance, I turn myself over to You." You will be as safe as the throne of God, for God is a faithful creator.

God Is Enough

A dollar is only worth as much as the government back of it. You buy a government bond and it is as secure as the government that stands behind it; but if it falls, your bond will be no good. Your bond, the currency of a country, is only as safe as the government of that country. Let the government fall and your bonds and your currency and everything else fall to the ground.

When I tell you, "Commit your soul to God in well doing, turn yourself over, take your hands off and deliver over to that higher power for keeping," then I have to qualify it by saying, "You will only be as safe as God. Is that safe enough for you?" If that is not enough, what can you add, where can you go, to whom can you turn? If God isn't enough, where do you look? But God is enough. In the words of "Te Deum Laudamus":

We praise thee, O God: we acknowledge thee
    to be the Lord.
All the earth doth worship thee: the Father everlasting.
To thee all Angels cry aloud: the Heavens, and all the
    Powers therein.
To the Cherubin and Seraphim: continually do cry
    Holy, Holy, Holy: Lord God of Sabaoth;
Heaven and earth are full of the Majesty: of thy glory.

If he isn't enough, better had we never been born. But God is enough. He upholds the heaven and the earth. I never tire of quoting from a Christian divine: "God is above all things, beneath all things, outside of all things, and inside of all things. God is above, but not pushed up. He is beneath, but He is not pushed down. He is outside, but not excluded. He is inside, but He is not confined. God is above all things presiding, beneath all things sustaining, outside all things embracing and inside all things filling."

This is the immanence of God. This is God. He is enough, so commit the keeping of your soul to the Creator. Turn yourself over to God through Jesus Christ and you will be all right.

16

THE CHRISTIAN DOESN'T HAVE A CARE IN THE WORLD

Casting all your care upon him; for he careth for you.

1 PETER 5:7

I have noticed that many Christians practice a common error concerning the promises of the Bible. Some have the tendency of including in one of God's promises something that He did not have in mind when He made it originally. People will read a promise in the Bible and assume that it applies to them.

For instance, it would be totally impossible to think of God saying this: "Casting all of your care upon him, you who are dead in trespasses and sins, who walk according to the course of this world, according to the prince of the power of the air, the spirit now worketh in the children of disobedience, you who walk in the lusts of the flesh fulfilling the desires of the flesh and of the mind and are by nature the children of wrath."

God could not possibly say in the same breath, "Cast all your cares upon me." He could not do it, He does not do it; and it is always a mistake to take a verse that does not belong to you and apply it to you. Or a verse that applies to anybody who meets a certain condition and you apply it to yourself if you have not met that condition. There is the error.

Suppose a letter came to your house and you opened it up rather carelessly and noticed that you had inherited $100,000. There would be a lot of human delight with the knowledge that you are well off, as men count such things. Upon closer examination, however, you notice that the letter had been opened by mistake after having been delivered by mistake. It belonged to a man with the same house number but another street. You could not possibly apply for that money; it was not yours, it was a mistake, you got the wrong mail. Therefore, when God says to certain ones, "Cast all your cares on me," you have to know whom He means. To whom is He addressing this? He is addressing it to the humble, the repentant, the believing, the obedient, the renewed and the elect.

One thing paramount throughout the Scriptures is that the Father's promises are for the Father's children, and we ought to keep that in mind. When the Jews, in Jesus' day, claimed certain promises for themselves because they were children of Abraham, Jesus said, "That's where you're mistaken. If you were children of Abraham you'd act like your father Abraham; but you're not children of Abraham, and all the promises made to Abraham were invalid and did not apply to these who were descendents of Abraham but not the seed of Abraham according to the spirit" (see Rom. 9:3-8; Gal. 3:15-29).

If it were not so tragic, it would be humorous to notice how politicians, newspapers and all the rest always seem to quote from the Bible when it is to their advantage when, in fact, their lifestyle is in a place where the Bible quotations cannot apply to them. This text is for God's children. Not for the prominent children of God only, or for the gifted or the successful. Many good Christians are not successful; many good saints are not prominent saints; and many wonderful people are not gifted people at all. God has given His gifts as He sees fit, sovereignly through nature and grace.

We tend to laud the gifted, the prominent and the successful. I do not know that God does. It is only faithfulness and love mentioned in the Scriptures and the willingness to give it all to Him. Apart from that, there is not much mention of success or prominence. So do not imagine that this does not apply to you just because you humbly say, "I'm not prominent or gifted or successful; I'm just one of the plain Christians." After all, so are we all before our heavenly Father; the weak and the struggling and obscure are just as dear to God as are the prominent and successful.

Dealing with Fears

Look a little at the presence of care in the world. Peter uses that word "care," and of course that means anxieties carried to the point of hidden fears. Fears and anxieties have a reason for existing. Being all optimism is irresponsible and unrealistic. Nobody can possibly be a sound judge of human affairs and be optimistic. All schemes to conquer fear by ignoring their cause are deceptive; and those who would follow them would be living in a paradise of fools. We cannot ignore the causes of our fears, because our fears are here and we have to admit their presence.

More than one million people each year die of malaria alone throughout the world. So there is illness everywhere throughout the world. And accidents occur among the good people along with illness and loss of jobs and betrayals and separations and bereavements and death and war. These things are loose in the earth.

The world is full of all this, and people are anxious and apprehensive, and we react variously when we are apprehensive. When scared, some people get very hardened. They develop a shell over them like a turtle's, hoping they can keep away the dangers they are afraid of, and they retire into that shell. Others drive themselves to achieve what they call success and become opulent, hoping they can buy their way through.

It was said of John D. Rockefeller before he died that he would give a million dollars for a good stomach. He lived on milk, crackers and a few easily digestible things because his stomach would not take solid food. The poorest farmer down in Tennessee can eat anything that he can chew and swallow, but this great man with all his millions could not get himself a stomach as good as a half-grown farm boy in the bog lands of Alabama.

Some people would go on and believe that they can stand off these fears by succeeding. However, you can succeed and have plenty, and still these fears creep in. You cannot buy off illness, and you cannot buy off accidents; and nobody can be so successful that he will not feel the war. Nobody can possibly be so high up in the world that he will not be a victim of betrayal or bereavement and, finally, illness and death.

Pleasure seeking is nothing else but a reaction to fear. "Eat, drink and be merry, for tomorrow we die." If I am going to die tomorrow, I might as well make good of it while I can and make what I can of life. So eat, drink and be merry today, for tomorrow that deadly thing appears, that fearful thing, death. That is the way some people act; they go wild. They do not want to face the anxieties, and so they go out and scatter anxieties for a little time by worldly pleasures. That is why if you can think of a new thing to please the people and make them play, then you can be sure of a lot of money.

Some people become nervous wrecks and have mental disorders of all kinds, all because they are scared. Is there anyone that can meet the enemies I have mentioned, and a thousand that I did not mention—illness and accidents and loss of job or possibility of it, betrayal, separation, bereavement, death—all these things; is there somebody that can meet these enemies? Somebody has to do it; they will not go away. Some believe that if we just ignore the enemy, it will all go away. Just pretend it does not exist is the foolish advice of some. These things do not go away by ignoring them. Illness does not go away when it is ignored.

A friend of my wife and I died recently of cancer. She was relatively young but she died. You can ignore it, but death will not go away; neither will war go, neither will accidents go away. You may cut it down a little by being careful, but the law of averages says that so many machines will break, so many people will fall asleep, so many reckless men will be on the highway. So these things will not go away.

The One Who Conquers Our Fears

Somebody has to face our fears and conquer them. Who is going to do it? You cannot do it. Is there somebody else who will take them on? Is there somebody else who will dispose of them? Is there someone who will say, "Now, listen, child of God, you're in the midst of a deadly world; death walks on every hand; car accident, mistakes, diseases, mental breaks, all these things walk up and down the land, but I'll take care of them for you. I do not promise you will not get into any of them, but I promise you do not have to be scared. I'll get you out of them, and I'll make them work for you, and I'll turn your evil to good, and I'll walk before them and I won't let one thing happen to you that isn't good for you; and when you need it, I'll let it happen, but I'll watch over you as a physician over his patient; I'll watch over you as a nurse over her child." Is there somebody who will say, "You do not have to be an optimist to ignore things; you can be a realist and admit their presence. And you don't have to collapse and be sent to an institution, I'll handle them for you"?

Yes, there is somebody: "Casting all your care upon him; for he careth for you." That is a sum of the Lord's Word to us on that subject. It is not all He said, but it is sort of a summation of it, and that same theme runs through the Old Testament and through the New Testament. The Savior teaches it and all the apostles teach it. It is simply that God is personally concerned about you. You, the individual, not the masses.

We think in masses and blocks. It is common to see graphs or charts in the news magazines that show a little figure standing in silhouette, in dark outline that stands for five million persons. The Lord never thinks in blocks and masses; He thinks in individuals. He thinks of His one sheep, of His one child.

That is the teaching of the Scriptures. God is personally concerned about you. God is not too high or lofty to remember that His children are in the land where illness is prevalent. Where accidents happen every day. Where there are loss of jobs and financial worries. Where people are betrayed by their closest loved ones. Where there is separation, as for instance, when the boy who has been close to us for so many years, shakes our hand with a grin that is not quite real and walks down the sidewalk and waves at the corner on his way to report to the military service. Separations come, some never to return to us again. God knows it and says, "Now, I know that's the kind of world you live in, but I have laid hold on you forever, and I know every detail of your trouble and all your problems, and I'll anticipate every act of the enemy and every act of every enemy I will anticipate. I will go before you." Not only will He go before us, but He also accepts our enemies as His enemies.

Our Enemy Is God's Enemy

"I will be an enemy to your enemies." Have you read that in your Bible? "But if thou shalt indeed obey his voice, and do all that I speak; then I will be an enemy unto thine enemies, and an adversary unto thine adversaries" (Exod. 23:22). That can mean only one thing: if an enemy turns on me, God turns on him. If I am partly in the wrong, God will let that enemy through to me enough to chasten me, but He will never let him destroy me. He will never let a blow fall that I do not deserve. Some great big strapping fellow would say good-naturedly, "Mother, you spanked me an awful lot when I was a boy." And the mother would dismiss it by saying, "You never got a lick amiss." In other words, "I never spanked you once too often."

Here were five great big handsome sons, doctors and what have you, sitting all around at homecoming, and here sat the mother presiding like a queen in the middle of it. They had all gone to college; they all had modern ideas, but they all still loved the woman, the old folks and mother. Never discussing how severe she was with them when they were boys and how she gave them the works occasionally, a great big friendly doctor said, "Mother, don't you think, after all, that you punished us a little too often?" She straightened up and said, "Young man, when you raise five such fine boys as I have, come back and talk to me." That was the answer.

God never strikes "a lick amiss," and He never lets anything happen to you if you're trusting that isn't good for you, and says, "Now, I'm handling this and you take your hands off and stop your worrying. This will not go away, but I will handle it and I will look after you, because I am personally concerned about you, and every enemy you have is My enemy too. You're on My side and I'm on your side, and the enemy's on the other side." God always handles the enemy.

"Cast all your care upon him." What are your cares? I do not know what your cares may be. I have given an outline of them here, and none of them may touch you at all. Maybe you are beset with worries that I have no remote notion that you feel; but the Bible says, "Cast all your care upon him."

Now this must be done at a given time by a firm act of the will. We do not just ooze into this or grow into it. If you were walking along and you had a great burden, and I said, "Let me carry that awhile," you would not shift that gradually over on to me. You would either give it to me or you would keep it. The act of transfer from you to me would be a crisis, an exact crisis that would happen at a given moment. One minute you had the burden, the other minute I had the burden.

When my father was a young man, he and some friend of his had somewhere to go, but they only had one horse. So my father's friend said, "I'll tell you what we'll do, Jake. I'll ride awhile and you can walk, then when you get tired, you can walk awhile and I'll ride."

My father, the country boy that he was, innocently agreed to that and that is the way it worked. The other fellow rode awhile and Jake walked; then after a while, Jake said, "Don't you think it's about time we ought to change off?"

"Oh, sure, getting tired," he said, "sure we'll change, and you can walk awhile, while I ride."

There is an awful lot of that same kind of arrangement among us Christians. We let God carry it awhile, we think, but He does not; we walk awhile and then we walk some more, and all our transfers are stymied. They do not go through; we do not make a complete transfer of our bargain. There was an old man that carried a 300-pound bag of grain on his shoulder while he was riding his mare, and somebody said, "Why don't you put the grain on the front of the horse's neck ahead of you?"

And he said, "She's got burden enough without carrying that, too; I'm a heavy man."

We carry our burden while God carries us as well as our burden. Why not be sensible and roll the burden off on God? If you are walking with the Lord, you are a humble person trusting in His grace, and you know that you are His child. This promise, then, is for you. Why should you not then roll your cares upon Him?

17

THE CHRISTIAN STANDS FIRM AGAINST FALSE TEACHING

Beloved, when I gave all diligence to write unto you of the common salvation, it was needful for me to write unto you, and exhort you that ye should earnestly contend for the faith which was once delivered unto the saints. For there are certain men crept in unawares, who were before of old ordained to this condemnation, ungodly men, turning the grace of our God into lasciviousness, and denying the only Lord God, and our Lord Jesus Christ.

JUDE 3-4

Peter, along with the other apostles, understood that the church faced an increasing array of false teaching and heresy. They knew by the whisper of the Holy Ghost within them that it was important to lay down a strong defense against false teaching and that the Christian needed to stand firm against everything that was not in harmony with the Scriptures. They needed to prepare the individual Christian to recognize false teaching and make a stand against it.

Much of the New Testament is given over to instructions in this regard. The apostle Paul spent a large amount of time writing along this line. Many of his epistles were written to combat some false teaching that had arisen in the church he had started.

An apostle that we do not hear very much about is Jude, a brother of Christ. He planned to write an encouraging letter, just as you might sit down to write your friends a letter of encouragement. He planned to write about what he called our "common salvation." But he was moved and impressed by the Holy Ghost to write something else altogether. An unpleasant circumstance had arisen, forcing him to write quite another kind of letter from the good encouraging letter he had planned. Certain men had crept into the fellowship unnoticed. Those men were men of evil personal lives and had been foreseen and condemned by the Lord Himself when He was with the disciples. They taught doctrine contrary to Christian faith. Jude writes to arouse the victims of these teachers to contend for the truth.

Seeing Things as They Truly Are

What do we mean by false teaching? It signifies teaching that things are otherwise than what they are. Both physical things and spiritual things are what they are. You can put a period after that. And when we have discovered or had revealed to us the facts about them, either things material or things spiritual, then we are morally required to acknowledge those facts and make our teachings conform to them. That is all so very simple that I almost apologize for saying it, but it is the broad framework upon which everything else must hang—that things are as they are. Whether we like them or not, that is the way they are. God made things, and things are. Physical and material things are and spiritual things are. It is our business to find out how they are, to accept them as they are and then make our teaching conform to them as they are.

Correct doctrine is of vital importance because it is simply the teaching of things as they are. Telling the truth about things is finding out what they are and then conforming my statement to their facts.

This is also so with spiritual truths. When a truth has been revealed in the Bible, our business is to find out what that truth is and then in all of our teaching conform to that truth—not edit it or change it, but let it stand just as it is. It is the truth of God declared as it is, and do not try to change it.

It would be ridiculous of me to try by some twist of logic or sophistry to make this be August when it's July, or to make it be the ninth when it's the third, or to make this be winter when it's summer, or to make this country to be Canada when it is the United States. Truth is just as it is. God Almighty made the world to be a mathematical universe and all things run according to mathematical laws. He has a moral world, which runs according to moral laws that are as exact and unchanging as His mathematical laws.

Nonconformity to the truth anywhere brings disaster. Let an engineer be wrong about a position, let him build according to that wrong concept and his building will collapse around him. Let a navigator be wrong about his calculations and he will run on a rock and his old ship will shudder as it runs onto a sandbar or a rock and will settle in the water and sink out of sight. The navigator has not gone according to truth. Nonconformity always brings disaster wherever it may be. And the vastness and hugeness of the disaster depend upon the high level or low level of the facts we have before us. False teaching is the falsifying of data about God, ourselves, sin and Christ.

A Wrong Idea About God

First, any false teaching must begin with the wrong concept of God. Nobody holding the right concept of God can go far wrong in anything else. And all the basic great mistakes that have been made, the great fundamental errors, have all rested down around concepts of God. Men are not willing to let God be what He says He is. They are always trying to change God and trying to make Him to be other than what He is.

God is, and we had better accept Him as He is. God is, and the angels want Him to be what He is. God is, and the elders, saints and heavenly creatures want Him to be what He is. We better want Him to be what He is and conform to what He is. Any structure or foundation that is crooked will bring the structure down in time. It will either sink or collapse or lean or fall over, but it will not stand long. Or if it does, it will lean as the leaning tower of Pisa in Italy.

Of all the foundations, God is the most important, because God is God and He made the heaven and earth and all the things therein. It would be a great error on the part of a man or woman to go a lifetime thinking they were talking to the God of heaven and earth and find they were talking to a god they had confounded out of their own imaginations.

For me to pray a lifetime and preach a lifetime about God in a way that was not true to what God is really would be a terrible, tragic calamity. To believe in a God that was a composite of ideas drawn from philosophy and psychology and other religions and superstitions would be eternally disastrous. No, God is what He is and we had better learn what God is and then conform our teachings to God.

Think of the attributes of God. They all comprise the nature of one God. If we eliminate or ignore any of those attributes, we come away with something that is less than God. For example, if you take all the justice, judgment and hatred of sin out of the nature of God, you have nothing left but a soft God. And those who have taken love and grace out end up with nothing but a God of judgment. Take away the personality of God and you have nothing but a mathematical God like the God of the scientists. All these are false, inadequate conceptions of God.

Our God is a God of justice and a God of grace; and while He is the God of righteousness, He also is the God of mercy. And while He is a God of mathematical exactness, He is also a God that could take babies in His arms and pat their heads and smile. He is a God that can forgive and a God that does forgive. So we had better make the study of this Bible the business of our lives to find out what God is and then conform our views to God.

A Wrong Idea About Ourselves

The second thing where we make a mistake is that any wrong idea of God is bound to give us a wrong idea of ourselves. Some people approach God through science and the study of anthropology; but anthropology without theology is bound to arrive at an error. You and I can only explain ourselves in the light of the doctrine that God made us out of the dust of the ground and blew into our nostrils the breath of life, and so man became a living soul. Science has discovered many things about God, but they have not discovered it in context. They have not begun with God and reason down to His world; they have begun with the world and tried to reason up to God and stop short of finding God. The result is tragic for everybody.

If man is wrong about God, then he is bound to be wrong about himself. If he is wrong about the artist, then he will be wrong about the picture. If he is wrong about the potter, then he will be wrong about the vessel. If he is wrong about God, then he will be wrong about the creature. While multiplying scientific facts all around us, which are wrong because they have left God out, they say there is no God. Or if there is a God, He is a God of mathematics and laws but not the God the Bible makes Him out to be. That is all wrong, and you cannot know the truth about yourself unless you first know the truth about God. You came from the hand of God, and back to God you must go for better, for worse, for judgment or for blessings.

So when we take God in, understand God and let God be what He claims to be, and believe about ourselves what God says about us, we are believing rightly. If you believe you are any better than God says you are, you are in error. If you believe you are any different from what God says you are, you are in error. You will falsify the data. Somebody has falsified the data and made you a victim. Believe about yourself what God says about you. Believe you are as bad as God says you are, and believe you are as far from Him as God says you are, and then believe in Christ who can come as near to Him as He says you can, and accept what He says about you as being truth.

A Wrong Idea About Sin

Then there is sin. Sin cannot be understood until we believe in God and believe what God has said about ourselves. Sin is that intrusive phenomenon, that ever-present, ubiquitous phenomenon. There it is—hatred, lies, dishonesty, murder, crime, dishonesty, justice, law, police, jails, locks and graves. But there are those who would deny it and, of course, that is falsifying the data. There are those who would rename sin, and they are falsifying the data. There are those who would treat it as a disease, and they are falsifying data.

God said that sin is a breaking of the law. God said it is rebellion against His will. God says that it is a nature inherited from our fathers and mothers. God says that it is an act against the faith and love and mercy of God. God says it is rebellion against constituted authority of the Majesty on High. God says it is iniquity and personally chargeable to the one who commits it. And God says, "The soul that sinneth, it shall die" (Ezek. 18:20). We had better believe about sin what God says about sin or we will be falsifying the data. Falsified data in spiritual things is more terribly wrong and will bring more terrible consequences then falsifying data in material things.

The doctor who miscounts the amount of a medicine that he gives a patient may kill the patient, which would be only to destroy a body. The preacher who misjudges or miscounts the truth concerning sin and man and God will damn his hearer, which is infinitely more terrible. Truth concerning God means I must accept God's sovereignty, God's holiness, God's justice, God's grace, God's love and all the Bible says about God. Concerning me, it requires that I must believe myself a fallen image of God, one who wants more of His image but fell short.

A Wrong Idea About Christ

Fourth is Christ Himself. For, if I do not have the right concept of God and of myself and of sin, then I will have a twisted and imperfect concept of Christ. I have no hesitation in saying that it is my honest and charitable conviction that the Christ of the average religion today is not the Christ of the Bible at all. He is a manufactured Christ, the Christ painted on canvas, the Christ drawn from cheap poetry, a Christ of the liberal and the soft and timid person. He is an imitation Christ that has not in Him the iron and the fury and the anger, as well as the love and grace and mercy. If I have a wrong conception of myself, I have a dangerous conception of sin. And if I have a dangerous conception of sin, I have a degraded conception of Christ.

Contend for the Truth

So here is the way it works. God is reduced and man is degraded and sin is underestimated and Christ is disparaged. No wonder the Jews said the terrible things they said. I recommend reading the book of Jude once. Get your teeth filed to a sharp eating edge, and then get your teeth into something substantial. Dare to believe something and dare to stand for God. In this awful day of so-called tolerance, people are ready to believe anything.

But ye, beloved, building up yourselves on your most holy faith, praying in the Holy Ghost, keep yourselves in the love of God, looking for the mercy of our Lord Jesus Christ unto eternal life. And of some have compassion, making a difference: And others save with fear, pulling them out of the fire; hating even the garment spotted by the flesh (Jude 20-23).

We are not called to smile and smile and smile. We are called sometimes to frown and rebuke with all long-suffering and doctrine. We must contend but not be contentious. We must preserve truth but injure no man. We must destroy error but not harm people. Some men were wrong in earlier days; they contended and, in contending, they became contentious. Trying to preserve truth, they destroyed those who held error. This is wrong. Let us preserve truth but injure no man. As Frederick W. Faber (1814-1863) writes in his hymn "Faith of Our Fathers":

Faith of our fathers, we will love
Both friend and foe in all our strife;
And preach Thee, too, as love knows how
By kindly words and virtuous life.

"Building up yourselves on your most holy faith." Are you these days building up yourselves? Have you read a book of the Bible through recently? Have you done any memorization of the Scriptures? Have you sought to know God? Are you looking to the radio and TV for your religion, or have you a Bible, and do you study it?

"*Praying in the Holy Ghost.*" I do not hesitate to say that most praying is not in the Holy Ghost. The reason we do not pray in the Holy Ghost is because we do not have the Holy Ghost in us. No man can pray in the Spirit except his heart is a habitation to the Spirit. It is only as the Holy Ghost has unlimited sway within us that we are able to pray in the Holy Ghost. I do not hesitate to say that five minutes of prayer in the Holy Ghost will be worth more than one year of mis-praying that is not in the Holy Ghost.

"*Keep yourselves in the love of God.*" Be true to the faith but be charitable to those who are in error. Never feel any contempt for anybody. No Christian has any right to feel contempt, for contempt is an emotion. It can only come out of pride, which is an open door for the enemy. So let us be an open tent; let us be charitable and loving through it all while we keep ourselves in the love of God. And, if we love God, we will also love God's.

"*Looking for the mercy of our Lord Jesus Christ unto eternal life.*" And of course, that is the second coming of Jesus, looking for Jesus Christ's coming. It is wonderful to me that His mercy will show itself at His coming. Even His mercy will show itself then as it did on the cross, as it does when receiving sinners, as it does in patiently looking after us Christians; and it will show itself at the coming of Jesus Christ unto eternal life.

"*Some have compassion, making a difference; And others save with fear, pulling them out of the fire; hating even the garment spotted by the flesh.*" There is a charge that we should win others, that we should do everything in our power to bring others to Christ, saving them with fear, pulling them out of the fire. John Wesley, all his life, referred to himself as the brand plucked from the burning.

He knew he was on fire, already he was in the hot flames of hell when Jesus Christ grabbed him out of the fiery pit, extinguished the fire by His own blood and Wesley became the Wesley we know. He never dared to rise and think of himself as a great Oxford man or a great genius, but always thought of himself as a brand plucked from the burning. And now we look forward to Jesus Christ's coming, looking for the mercy of our Jesus Christ. Here was what the old silk weaver Gerhard Tersteegen (1697–1769) said about Christ:

> There is a balm for every pain,
> A medicine for all sorrow;
> The eye turned backward to the Cross,
> And forward to the morrow.

Some of the old saints in days gone by called the Communion service, medicine of immortality. You could not follow them in every one of their beliefs, but in that I think they were right. Medicine for all sorrow, an eye turned backward to the cross and forward to the morrow. The morrow of the glory and the song when He shall come. The morrow of the harping and the balm and the welcome home.

Meantime, in His beloved hand are ways.

Meantime, what are we going to do? Give up to the heat?

Meantime, what are we going to do? Give up to the liberals?

Meantime, what are we going to do? Give up to the dead church?

Meantime, what are we going to do? Give up to those who have chosen to walk in the low shadow of Christianity?

Never!

Dare to contend without being contentious. Dare to preserve truth without hurting people. Dare to love and be charitable and, meantime, there is rest and comfort for the weary one who lays his head upon His breast.

Let us by the grace of God, with charity for all and hatred for none, but determination to be loyal to truth if it kills us, put our chin a little higher and our knees a little lower, and let's look a little further into the throne of God, for Jesus Christ sits at the right hand of God the Father Almighty. And let us be courageous, attentive, severe but kind. Let us pray in the Holy Ghost, keep ourselves in the love of God, build ourselves up in the most holy faith and win all we can until the day of the glory and the song.

Amen.

Follow Tozer's new writings on Twitter at
http://twitter.com/tozeraw